"The General Epistles conti
church's detriment. This bo
does so in a winsome and very helpful fashion. Written for a broader audience, it evidences the sound and careful scholarship from which any interested reader will benefit. This volume will make an excellent resource for personal and group Bible study. I commend it most highly."

—**Richard B. Gaffin Jr.**, Professor of Biblical and Systematic Theology, Emeritus, Westminster Theological Seminary

"These essays are an excellent way to begin the study of the seven Catholic Epistles. They orient the reader to the most important themes and aspects of the books and resolve many of the difficult questions that Christians often have about them. Crowe has a way of gently disentangling thorny interpretative issues and exposing the spiritual fruit for believers to harvest. This is what 'practical theology' ought to be. Readers will learn not only the distinctive teachings of each of these New Testament epistles but also how each one clarifies and personalizes the indicatives and imperatives of our faith. Each chapter ends with a set of questions to guide readers and groups to deeper reflection on the saving message of each biblical book."

—**Charles E. Hill**, John R. Richardson Professor of New Testament and Early Christianity, Reformed Theological Seminary, Orlando

"Too often the letters at the end of the canon, which are often called the Catholic Epistles, are neglected. We ignore these letters to our peril, for they have an urgent message for the church today. Crowe faithfully expounds these letters in a brief and accessible manner. In unpacking the message of the Catholic Epistles, he demonstrates how they are an essential part of the gospel message. Pastors, students, and all others interested in the message of the Scriptures will benefit from this theologically faithful and pastorally applicable work.":

—**Thomas R. Schreiner**, James Buchanan Harrison Professor of New Testament Interpretation and Associate Dean, The Southern Baptist Theological Seminary

"Peter, John, James, Jude—important early-church leaders who knew Jesus and wrote letters to churches. Why do we neglect them? This book uncovers the treasure hidden in these passed-over writings. In a survey that is terse and gripping, Brandon Crowe shows how, in turbulent times not unlike ours, God furnished direction for his people and light for the world. The book's stress on God and Jesus reinforces the truth that the General Epistles, like all the rest of Scripture, point beyond humans and their situations to the divine wisdom that is transforming the world—and that can change our lives."

—**Robert W. Yarbrough**, Professor of New Testament, Covenant Theological Seminary

The
MESSAGE *of the*
GENERAL EPISTLES
in the HISTORY
of REDEMPTION

The MESSAGE *of the* GENERAL EPISTLES *in the* HISTORY *of* REDEMPTION

WISDOM FROM JAMES, PETER, JOHN, AND JUDE

BRANDON D. CROWE

P U B L I S H I N G
P.O. BOX 817 • PHILLIPSBURG • NEW JERSEY 08865-0817

Unless otherwise indicated, all Scripture quotations are from the ESV® Bible (The Holy Bible, English Standard Version®), copyright © 2001 by Crossway, a publishing ministry of Good News Publishers. Used by permission. All rights reserved. All quotations are from the 2007 text edition of the ESV.

Scripture quotations marked (NIV) are from the HOLY BIBLE, NEW INTERNATIONAL VERSION®. NIV®. Copyright © 1973, 1978, 1984, 2011 by International Bible Society. Used by permission of Zondervan Publishing House. All rights reserved.

Italics within Scripture quotations indicate emphasis added.

ISBN: 978-1-62995-051-8 (pbk)
ISBN: 978-1-62995-052-5 (ePub)
ISBN: 978-1-62995-053-2 (Mobi)

Printed in the United States of America

Library of Congress Cataloging-in-Publication Data

Crowe, Brandon D.
 The message of the General Epistles in the history of redemption : wisdom from James, Peter, John, and Jude / Brandon D. Crowe. -- 1st ed.
    pages cm
 Includes bibliographical references and index.
 ISBN 978-1-62995-051-8 (pbk.)
 1. Bible. Catholic Epistles--Criticism, interpretation, etc. I. Title.
 BS2777.C76 2015
 227'.906--dc23
                    2014033935

To my parents,
for their unwavering love and support

Contents

FOREWORD

AS I READ THROUGH this book by my colleague, I was struck by how relevant the General Epistles are to our own day. In these New Testament letters, warnings abound against heresies and against enticements to immorality. In the first century, people rose up and claimed to be Christian but furnished various excuses for why it was all right to descend into immoralities. Excuses are still being manufactured today.

We need a book such as this one to remind us of principles of godliness. We need it all the more because some of the messages in the General Epistles are not only relevant but unpopular, given the atmosphere in the mainstream of modern Western cultures.

The modern atmosphere will tell us that love and tolerance unite us, while doctrine divides us. Attention to doctrine allegedly makes us "dogmatic." Rejection of someone else's views makes us "intolerant." In contrast to this modern antipathy to truth, the General Epistles combat and denounce false doctrine in no uncertain terms. They tell us that sound doctrine is not optional but necessary, and that it is our duty as followers of Christ to reject the soul-destroying doctrines of heretics. They call us to commend true doctrine out of love for Christ and love for our fellow human beings, whose souls are in danger from heresy.

The modern atmosphere will also tell us that obeying biblical instructions for ethical behavior is "inhibiting" and "puritanical" and "oppressive." Modern thinking alleges that when we teach biblical moral standards, we show ourselves not only to be behind the times, but to be destroyers of human flourishing—haters of the human race. We also hear voices and see practices *within* the Christian community that tell us not to teach or enforce certain moral standards—especially, it seems, in sexual ethics—because we will allegedly destroy bridges to pagans and opportunities to proclaim the gospel, and we ourselves will become legalists rather than proclaimers of free grace. By contrast, the General Epistles warn us vigorously against all kinds of libertinism and against all kinds of excuses for falling into the ways of the world.

Of course, as usual, there is a grain of truth to be found in accusations from the modern atmosphere. It is indeed possible to substitute legalism for the true gospel. It is likewise possible to quarrel continually about minor points in doctrine, and to conduct disputes in a spirit of pride and anger rather than love. We have all the more need for hearing and studying biblical instruction concerning true doctrine and false, and concerning true morality and false.

An author writing about the General Epistles confronts challenges. For one thing, these books of the New Testament form quite a diverse collection. They have a number of different human authors; they address a number of quite distinct situations; and their contents vary widely in topic. So digesting and applying them requires care. In addition, we face the fact that, along with the similarities between then and now, there are also dissimilarities. The situations differ. The heresies and temptations that confronted God's people in the first century are not always identical with those today. Yet they are *relevant* to today.

My colleague Brandon Crowe is well qualified to lead readers through the ins and outs. God has gifted him as a teacher. He knows how to prioritize what is important. He explains the main themes of these letters simply and clearly. At the same time, he explains the contents of these letters in a way that draws our attention to their importance for our own day. I take pleasure in recommending this book to the public.

Vern S. Poythress
Professor of New Testament Interpretation,
Editor of the *Westminster Theological Journal*,
Westminster Theological Seminary

PREFACE

THIS BOOK IS WRITTEN FOR the nonspecialist, and is an invitation to consider the theological richness and practical relevance of the books of James, 1–2 Peter, 1–3 John, and Jude. I hope that it will be a book that can be used in a variety of settings, from church groups to the classroom. Extensive footnotes, foreign languages, and technical jargon have been kept to a minimum, though I do hope to introduce some aspects from these biblical texts that may be less familiar.

Much of this book grows out of a course on the General Epistles taught at Westminster Theological Seminary, and I am grateful to the students for their many insightful questions and comments that have helped my own understanding of these texts. I continue to benefit greatly from the knowledge of my colleagues at Westminster Seminary, especially New Testament colleagues Dr. Vern Poythress, who provided valuable feedback on an earlier draft of the manuscript, and Dr. Greg Beale. I received informal feedback on the topics discussed in this volume from many along the way, though any shortcomings remain my own. I would also like to acknowledge my indebtedness to Dr. Charles E. Hill, who first introduced me to the academic study of these New Testament documents some years ago, and whose teaching has been formative for my own understanding of these texts. I am grateful to the board and administration of Westminster Seminary, who generously provide the resources and support necessary to undertake projects such as this one. Special thanks goes to the staff of the Montgomery Library for going the extra mile on various occasions. I would also like to thank everyone at P&R Publishing who has so capably assisted in the production of this volume, including John J. Hughes, Amanda Martin, and Karalee Reinke.

Last, but by no means least, I would like to thank my family. Our children, Charlie, Simeon, and Ethan, have provided many joyful interruptions from writing, and they are tremendous blessings in the quiver. Singular thanks are due to my wife, Cheryl—my best friend and coheir of the grace of life (1 Peter 3:7). I dedicate this volume to my parents, Doug and Rhonda Crowe, for their indefatigable love, support, and encouragement as far back as I can remember. I owe them an incalculably great debt, and thank God for them.

Introduction

Why This Book?

In our study of the Bible, it can be easy to focus on certain portions and neglect others. This imbalance is normally not for any lack of good intention, but life is busy and there is plenty to keep us occupied in the longer and more familiar books of the Bible. Unfortunately, this can mean that we often miss some important insights into the nature of salvation and how Christians should live in today's world in light of the work of Christ. One portion of the Bible that is often overlooked is the New Testament collection often called the *General Epistles*,[1] or what one might call "the rest of the New Testament": James, 1–2 Peter, 1–3 John, and Jude. These seven letters are all brief (three of them are only one chapter long), and they are tucked away at the end of the New Testament between the longer books Hebrews and Revelation.

Additionally, it is not surprising that many of these letters are neglected since their teaching can be difficult to understand. Why does James say that we are justified by works and not by faith alone (James 2:24)? How does this relate to what the apostle Paul says, when he states emphatically that we are justified by faith in Jesus Christ and not by works of the law (Gal. 2:16)? Who are the spirits that Christ preached to in prison, and how

---

1. This term simply refers to letters written for more general purposes when compared, for example, to Paul's letters that are addressed to specific churches. Sometimes these are called *Catholic Epistles*, which simply means "universal epistles," and is not a reference to the Roman Catholic Church.

does this relate to Noah (1 Peter 3:19–20)? Why does Peter mention angels kept in chains in gloomy darkness (2 Peter 2:4), and how is this supposed to impact us today? What is Jude's point in recounting the archangel Michael's contending with the devil about the body of Moses (Jude 9)? Why does John say that if we are really followers of Christ, we do not sin (1 John 3:6)? Don't we all continue to sin every day? These are a few of the questions that may arise when reading the rest of the New Testament.

In light of the challenges that these books pose and the relative lack of attention devoted to them, the purpose of this volume is to help us understand what each of these books teaches about the salvation accomplished by Christ, and how this relates to life. Indeed, one of the striking features of these books is how relevant they are today. They are written after the coming of Christ—after his incarnation, ministry, death, resurrection, and ascension—and reflect on his work and teaching for the early church communities. These churches were made up of people just like us, and it turns out that they faced problems that are not too different from things we face in the twenty-first century. They dealt with social ostracism—and perhaps worse—because of their faith in a crucified and resurrected man and because of their distinctive way of living in this world. They were confronted with those who opposed their traditional beliefs about Jesus, especially the "outdated" notion that Jesus was coming back. Many teachers in the church were more interested in money, sex, and the acclamation of others than with genuine love for Christ and the true gospel. They were confronted with splits in the church from those who were espousing a supposedly better way to think about theology and life than what the apostles taught. The early Christians faced real dilemmas; they often struggled to understand their identity in a world that did not share their convictions. This is why the apostles wrote urgently to them to ensure that they understood the sufficiency of Christ's work, and how we are to live faithfully in light of it. These letters explain important aspects of the gospel of grace and warn us against real dangers of distorting that gospel. We neglect the rest of the New Testament at our own peril.

We will see that these letters often explain the work of Christ in unique ways, though always in accord with what we find elsewhere in the Bible. By focusing both on the work of Christ for us and on the calls to discipleship in these letters, we will also gain a greater vision for how we are to live in this present age. Stated another way, these letters provide a great opportunity to consider the relationship between the indicative and imperative in the Bible. Simply stated, the *indicative* refers to the saving work of God in Christ on our behalf. The *imperative* assumes and logically follows the indicative, and entails commands for how to live. It is important to recognize the indicative-imperative theological structure because it helps us keep in proper perspective the relationship between the definitive accomplishment of salvation and the Bible's very real call to Christian obedience. The primacy of the indicative keeps us from thinking that our works ever make us righteous before God. The necessity of the imperative means that we are not free to disregard the clear commands of Scripture, even though we are saved freely by grace alone.[2]

Allow me to emphasize two things about the indicative-imperative relationship as it relates to the present book. First, the order of the two cannot be switched: the indicative must precede the imperative. The foundation for our salvation and acceptance with God is always the work of Christ, and never from anything that we do. This point cannot be overstressed. In terms of being made right with God (justification), we can

2. For further discussion on the indicative-imperative relationship in the General Epistles, see G. K. Beale, *A New Testament Biblical Theology: The Unfolding of the Old Testament in the New* (Grand Rapids: Baker Academic, 2011), 851–56.

do nothing that would add any righteousness to our status before God. To treat commands as if they were the means by which we could earn our salvation would be an egregious perversion of the gospel of salvation by grace through faith. The Bible makes it clear that God sought us when we did not seek him, even while we were dead in our sins (see, among many others, Rom. 5:8; Eph. 2:4-9; 1 John 4:10). Therefore, the ability for us truly to please God by obedience is dependent on the application of the redemption accomplished by Christ to each of us personally, and this comes by faith, not by our works. We often see this indicative-imperative relationship reflected even in the structure of biblical books, as biblical authors articulate the work of Christ before giving practical exhortations. This basic structure is evident, for example, in Romans (indicative: Rom. 1-11; imperative: Rom. 12-16) and Ephesians (indicative: Eph. 1-3; imperative: Eph. 4-6), but we even see it in the Old Testament with books such as Deuteronomy (for example, Deut. 6:20-25). Even where an imperative may be given before an explicit statement about the indicative, the indicative remains logically prior to the imperative. In this spirit, our study of each letter among the General Epistles will begin by considering what each states about the salvation accomplished by Christ.

The second important aspect of the indicative-imperative relationship is that the indicative and imperative can never be separated. In other words, the gospel entails legitimate calls to Christian obedience that are founded on the work of Christ (see Phil. 2:12-13). Indeed, we can even say that there is no salvation without accompanying discipleship. Put in theological terms, justification (being made right with God definitively) and sanctification (the process of growing in holiness) are always a package deal. Thus, although our good works can never secure us a right standing before God, we are not saved without the fruit of good works (see Eph. 2:10 in light of Eph. 2:8–9). The necessity of good works for salvation may seem to contradict the free grace of the gospel, yet it simply means that faith alone saves, but the faith that saves is never alone. A denial of this crucial theological point may be in the background of several of the letters we will consider in this book. It appears that too many in the early church were wrongly teaching and living in a way that proclaimed that the call to holiness for Christians is (at best) optional, and that we have no responsibility to live in accord with God's standards. As we will see, however, it is clear that God requires holiness among his people—even among those who are saved by the righteousness of Christ. I will have much more to say on this point in due course.

Thus, we can never add any value to the completed, sufficient work of Christ, but we must take the biblical commands seriously. The good news is that the false teachers were wrong about what brings liberty: freedom comes not by following the sinful desires of one's own heart, but through the liberating grace of God. Indeed, James has much to say about the law *of liberty*. As we progress through each of these letters, focusing on both the indicative and the imperative, I pray that we will appreciate the freeing and enlivening benefits of grace in a new way.

Scallywags, Scoffers, and Schisms: Understanding the Structure of This Book

Maybe you have picked up this book and are still reading simply because you want to understand the meaning of the titles for the book's first three parts. Perhaps you are wondering: how do the terms *scallywags*, *scoffers*, and *schisms* relate to this portion of the New Testament? I have chosen these alliterative (and, I hope, memorable) terms to help us organize our thinking about some of the main contributions of each of these letters.

Scallywags

Scallywags refers to the way in which the world views Christians, according to 1 Peter. A scallywag is a rogue, a troublemaker, a good-for-nothing person who is (or, in the case of 1 Peter, seems to be) causing problems. In 1 Peter, Christians are faced with difficult circumstances and various sorts of opposition, but they are called to demonstrate by their manner of life, as they follow the selfless pattern of Christ himself, that they are anything but scallywags. First Peter makes it clear that when Christians are living faithfully, they support the public good and are above disrepute and dishonor. In other words, Christians are to disprove the charge of being scallywags by living in accord with the gospel.

Scoffers

The title of this book's second part focuses on 2 Peter and Jude. Here we find that many *scoffers* will arise and distort the true teaching of Scripture. We will also see that when false teaching as described in 2 Peter and Jude holds sway, it leads not simply to scoffing at theological propositions, but also to scoffing at the call to discipleship and the call to be holy as God is holy.

Schisms

Schisms is a term that might refer to any number of books or issues in the New Testament, but understanding schisms is particularly important for interpreting 1 John. This epistle may seem to contain many confusing or troublesome statements, but we will see that part of what John was addressing was schisms, or divisions, arising in the early church, led by those who did not follow the apostolic teaching. These schismatics had their own ideas about what makes one spiritual, and they eventually left the church. Thus, we will consider how recognizing the schisms in the background of John's writings helps us understand the teaching of 1–3 John as it relates to us today.

Wisdom for Life

Finally, we will consider how the teaching of James, the brother of Jesus, helps us navigate life in this present age. We will certainly consider what James has to say about the indicative of salvation (he says more than we may realize at first glance), but we will also consider the way James reflects on the teachings of Jesus with a view to helping Christians live well as we await Jesus' return.

Moving Forward

I think you will find that there is much to glean about the nature of salvation in James, 1–2 Peter, 1–3 John, and Jude. At the same time, we will see that the biblical authors wrote to help the church navigate some tricky issues, many of which are still with us today. In terms of reading strategy, it will be helpful to read each biblical book before reading the corresponding chapters in this volume. It will also be helpful to read the biblical texts, as much as possible, in one sitting to be attuned to the overall flow of the texts. Questions for reflection and discussion are included at the end of each chapter. You may want to read these after (or possibly before) each chapter to help stimulate your thinking.

May God grant that all of us will see more clearly and deeply the depths of his love in Christ, and enable us by his grace to love and serve him and those around us with greater faithfulness. To this end, let us now embark on our study of these important New Testament letters.

Questions for Reflection and Discussion

1. Have you read any of the letters of James through Jude before? If so, what do you remember? What may have been difficult or confusing about them?

2. What does the *indicative* of salvation refer to, generally speaking?

3. What does the *imperative* of salvation refer to, generally speaking?

4. What two points are necessary to remember about the relationship between the indicative and the imperative?

Abbreviations

ACCSNT	Ancient Christian Commentary on Scripture: New Testament
BECNT	Baker Exegetical Commentary on the New Testament
BST	Bible Speaks Today
EBT	Explorations in Biblical Theology
ESV	English Standard Version
JETS	*Journal of the Evangelical Theological Society*
NAC	New American Commentary
NACSBT	New American Commentary Studies in Bible and Theology
NICNT	New International Commentary on the New Testament
NIV	New International Version
NSBT	New Studies in Biblical Theology
NTC	New Testament Commentary [Baker]
PNTC	Pillar New Testament Commentary
PPS	Popular Patristics Series
TNTC	Tyndale New Testament Commentary

WBC	Word Biblical Commentary
WCF	Westminster Confession of Faith
WLC	Westminster Larger Catechism
WSC	Westminster Shorter Catechism
WTJ	*Westminster Theological Journal*

Part 1

SCALLYWAGS

I

An Eternal Inheritance: Salvation in 1 Peter

Blessed be the God and Father of our Lord Jesus Christ! According to his great mercy, he has caused us to be born again to a living hope through the resurrection of Jesus Christ from the dead, to an inheritance that is imperishable, undefiled, and unfading. (1 Peter 1:3–4a)

But you are a chosen race, a royal priesthood, a holy nation, a people for his own possession, that you may proclaim the excellencies of him who called you out of darkness into his marvelous light. (1 Peter 2:9)

[Jesus] himself bore our sins in his body on the tree, that we might die to sin and live to righteousness. By his wounds you have been healed. (1 Peter 2:24)

AS WE BOARDED the train in Paris that January evening, it was already getting dark. Along with four friends, I was on my way to Normandy to visit the famous D-Day beaches where the

Allied troops had landed in Europe during World War II. Being entrusted with the map, I was fairly certain I knew where we were going, and the appropriate station at which to disembark, but backpacking through Europe is not always a precise science. We had no hotel reservations, we had no plan of transportation once we got off the train, and none of us spoke French very well. (I might add that this was before the days of ubiquitous smartphones and GPS devices.) As we had already done on a number of occasions, we were planning on walking a short distance from the train station until we found suitable lodging for the night. When we stepped into the darkness of rural France, however, we could see little, aside from the train heading methodically down the rails to its next destination. We were on our own.

We headed in the direction where we surmised the closest town must be, but there were no landmarks, no lights, and apparently no end in sight. After what seemed like an hour, we finally found a building with the lights on. We stopped and asked directions, only to discover that the language was a significant barrier. After doing our best to translate the directions we received, we resumed our journey, but found ourselves back at the same place some time later! It was a frustrating and desperate feeling. When we eventually found a hotel, it was much nicer than anything we were used to. Despite the cost, we booked our rooms right away. When I removed my backpack that evening, the burden that was lifted was as much psychological as physical. We had finally made it to a haven of rest after being lost in the darkness of a foreign country.

Perhaps you have had a similar experience. It is an unsettling feeling to be in a strange place and not know what to do next. In many respects, this was the situation facing the first readers of 1 Peter. Peter wrote this letter to Christians who had very likely been displaced from their homes and transplanted in a foreign land far away from all that was familiar. But they were also navigating a more fundamental issue, one that all Christians can identify with. The recipients of the letter found themselves professing a faith in a world that did not understand their convictions, which often led to pressures and persecutions. As we will see in this chapter, however, Peter wrote to encourage Christians with the immeasurable love of God directed toward them, even in the midst of their difficult circumstances. Although his readers were facing the vicissitudes of uncertainty, Peter explains that a glorious reward, one that is eternally secure, is laid up in heaven for them. In this chapter, we will primarily consider the theological underpinnings of Peter's message; in the next chapter, we will see how a solid grasp of the love of God for us in Christ empowers us to live faithfully in the present age, even in the face of fiery trials.

Elect Exiles: The Audience of 1 Peter

The Historical Context of Exile

The apostle Peter addresses his first epistle to the elect exiles of the Dispersion in various portions of what is called Asia Minor (modern-day Turkey): Pontus, Galatia, Cappadocia, Asia, and Bithynia. Who were these people, and why were they described as *exiles*? Although we cannot be certain of all the historical details, the audience may have comprised Christians who had left Rome behind to be resettled in these Roman provinces.[1] If so, they may have gone to Asia Minor willingly, with the prospect of new opportunities. But it is more likely that they would have been forced to leave Rome because they were viewed as foreigners who were a threat to the order of Rome. We know, for example, that the emperor Claudius (reigned A.D. 41–54) established Roman

1. On the historical situation of 1 Peter, I largely follow Karen H. Jobes, *1 Peter*, BECNT (Grand Rapids: Baker Academic, 2005), 28–41.

cities in all five of the provinces mentioned in 1 Peter 1:1. We also know that Claudius was zealous for traditional Roman religion, and he expelled Jews from Rome in the A.D. 40s (see Acts 18:2). The Roman historian Suetonius, writing in the early second century A.D., even connects the expulsion of Jews from Rome to a certain *Chrestus*, which may be a misspelling of *Christus*, the Latin word for *Christ*.[2] If so, Claudius's deportations of Jews may also have included Christians. (In the early days of Christianity, it was often difficult for outsiders to distinguish between Christians and Jews.)

Thus, it is quite plausible that Christians may have been forced to leave Rome because of their religious beliefs. If so, it may also be true that these deportees would not have officially been Roman citizens, even if they and their families had lived in Rome for generations. This would leave them in the uncomfortable situation of being a people without a homeland: though they were living in Rome, their lack of Roman citizenship meant that they had to leave behind the only place that many of them probably ever knew as home. When they were resettled in Asia Minor, they were also viewed as outsiders by the local populaces. If this historical reconstruction is correct, then the audience may quite literally have been exiles without a homeland.

To make matters worse, even though the political and religious pressures of the city of Rome may have been left behind, the exiles were not free from religious, political, or social pressures in Asia Minor. There would have been immense pressure for the dispersed Christians to conform to local religious and cultural customs; failure to do so would have led to antagonism and accusations. For example, if Christians were abstaining from worshiping traditional deities who were thought to bless Rome, then they would have been considered to be unpatriotic

2. Suetonius, *Claudius* 25.4.

scallywags.[3] (In ancient Rome, religion and society were closely intertwined in ways that may strike many today, especially in the United States, as foreign.) How, then, could Christians live faithfully in a society that did not understand—much less abide by—Christian beliefs? Christians were viewed as immoral (their lifestyles did not accord with the broader culture, see 1 Peter 3:16; 4:4) and atheistic (Christians denied the traditional pantheon of gods).[4] The word *Christian* was even used in the early days of the church as a derogatory term (4:14, 16). Peter writes in the midst of this anti-Christian context, making it clear to his audience of Christians that they should supply no ground to the charge of being scallywags. As we will see in the next chapter, Christians are to be model citizens, paragons of patience, and steadfast in their love (2:15; 3:9, 13, 16).

Exile in Scripture

Whatever the details of the historical situation in 1 Peter, the theological message of elect exiles is clear. Exile is an important theme in Scripture. In the Old Testament, exile is set forth as the preeminent covenantal curse if God's people turned aside to other gods and forsook the Lord (Lev. 26:27–39; Deut. 28:25–68). Exile meant that God's people were expelled from the Promised Land and were subject to pagan kings who had no desire to live according to God's law. To be in exile would be to hit rock bottom. As the Old Testament unfolds, we find that the Assyrians conquered the northern kingdom of Israel (2 Kings 17), and the Babylonians took the Judahites into exile, even burning down Solomon's temple (2 Kings 25). These passages show us that, tragically, the covenantal curse of exile did become a reality for God's people.

3. See Robert Louis Wilken, *The Christians as the Romans Saw Them*, 2nd ed. (New Haven, CT: Yale University Press, 2003).

4. See Paul J. Achtemeier, *1 Peter: A Commentary on First Peter*, Hermeneia (Minneapolis: Fortress, 1996), 28–36.

Exile, however, is not the last word of the Old Testament. Isaiah prophesied a future overcoming of the exile and blessings for God's people (Isa. 40–66). We go on to read that after the Persians conquered the Babylonians, Persian King Cyrus allowed the Israelites to return to their homeland and even paid their way (2 Chron. 36:22; Ezra 1)! Their return led to the rebuilding of Jerusalem's walls (Nehemiah) and the rebuilding of the temple (Ezra). The return from exile was a promising prospect for God's people, but the fullness of eschatological blessings that the prophets had foretold would come after the end of exile did not immediately come to fruition. The rebuilt temple was not as impressive as Solomon's temple. No king was on the throne in Jerusalem. God's people still struggled to live in covenantal faithfulness. After the prophet Malachi, who anticipates the return of Elijah, Israel endured around 400 years of silence and uncertainty. Was the exile really over, if the full blessings of the return from exile had not yet been experienced?

Enter Matthew's genealogy (Matt. 1:1–17). It may seem like a boring read to many today, but that may be because we do not understand the gravity of the darkness facing God's people in the days before Jesus came, and the corresponding anticipation for the coming king to occupy the throne of David. If the exile was over, where was the king? In reality, there was no legitimate Davidic king on the throne of Israel (Herod the Great was merely a squatter). In this context, Jesus is introduced as the Son of Abraham (he is descended from the fountainhead of Israel) and Son of David (he is the true King). Following the ministry of John the Baptist (who had come in the spirit and power of Elijah in accord with Malachi), Jesus embarked on a kingly ministry and defeated the enemies that oppressed God's people. Indeed, John the Baptist's ministry of preparation is explained by a prominent Old Testament passage that heralds the ultimate end of exile and a new day of salvation (Isa. 40:3).

The way in which Jesus brought salvation, however, was surprising. The Messiah was generally expected to be a king who would conquer the Roman Empire. Yet Jesus was put to death on a Roman cross! Was Jesus not the conquering King? Indeed he was (and is)! Whereas many of Jesus' contemporaries considered the Roman occupiers to be the primary enemy, Jesus fought a deeper, more significant battle primarily against sin and the kingdom of darkness. To be sure, Jesus' work has all sorts of ramifications for the rule of Rome (as we will see in 1 Peter), but Jesus did not come merely to topple Rome; he came to conquer the devil, sin, and even death (1 John 3:8). Jesus conquered the root of the problem.

How does all this relate to exile? Jesus preached the kingdom of God and showed himself to be the true King of Jerusalem in accord with Scripture (Zech. 9:9; Matt. 21:5). He spoke a word of judgment against the temple of his day, declaring himself to be the true Temple, and became the One who would reverse the curse on his people by undergoing the curse of death himself (Deut. 21:23; Gal. 3:13). The coming of the true King from the line of David and his substitutionary cursing brought the end of the exile and the beginning of the age of the fulfillment of God's blessings. Central to the age of blessing is the outpouring of the Spirit, which was anticipated by the Old Testament prophets (Joel 2:28–32). The prophets also anticipated the making of a new covenant (Jer. 31:31–34), the unification of God's people under one king (Ezek. 37:15–28), and the establishment of an everlasting kingdom (Isa. 9:6–7; Dan. 2:44). These are the blessings of the last days, which Peter indicates we are already beginning to experience, since we live in the last days (1 Peter 1:20). Yet the perfect experience of these blessings is yet to come. This tension is what theologians often call the *already* and *not yet* structure of New Testament eschatology (with *eschatology* meaning that we are now living in the latter days of blessing anticipated by

Scripture). Although the curse of the exile is already over for God's people because of the work of Jesus the Messiah, difficulties and hardships remain.

This brief survey of exile serves to show that the exile of the Christians in 1 Peter is not to be equated with the covenantal curses from the Old Testament, but refers more to the reality that there is a *not yet* to the perfect experience of God's blessings. We await the consummation of the kingdom of God that will occur when Christ returns. Yet we also must not neglect Peter's emphasis that we are already experiencing the benefits of living in the age of fulfillment.

Despite the melancholic imagery that the exile evokes, the term *exiles* is also a designation for God's true people in the midst of a foreign, ungodly society. By using this term, Peter connects his audience (who may have been mainly Gentiles) to the people of God in the Old Testament by focusing on their shared experience of exile. The way in which Peter uses this scriptural topos has significant implications for how we understand the church's relationship to Israel in the New Testament. Peter is telling us here that the church—made up of both Jew and Gentile—is heir to the Old Testament promises. He will return to this point throughout the letter.

Therefore, the term *exiles*, while perhaps reflecting the actual situation of the original audience, is the perfect metaphor for Peter to use to explain the relationship of Christians to the unbelieving world. Peter picks up on this theme for his readers in 1:1, 17; 2:11, and even refers to himself as an exile by writing from "Babylon" (5:13), which is probably a covert reference to Rome,[5] since Babylon was the quintessential place of exile in the Old Testament. By focusing on the theme of exile in these ways, Peter instructs his readers that they will not be comfortable in this world. In fact, they should expect

---

5. *Babylon* also seems to be referring to Rome on some level in Revelation 16–18.

opposition, because this present world, as it now exists, is not their true home.

God's Love for Exiles

Peter not only reminds the readers that they are exiles, but refers to them as *elect* exiles. This is a significant juxtaposition of terms. Their status as elect, in addition to connecting them to God's elect people in the Old Testament (Deut. 7:6–8), is a way to assure the readers of God's love for them. Perhaps some reading this book consider election to be a controversial topic. Yet we should recognize that election is a biblical term. The Bible uses the concept of election to encourage us that God is at work in us even before we seek him. Election should encourage us that our salvation is God's work and God's blessing to us. Election is not intended to discourage us, force us to engage in impossible guessing games about God's secret decree, or entrap us in fearful introspection. Election is an eminently practical doctrine that should cause us to look outside ourselves to the priority of God's action in salvation—action that God took even before we were born! God's election is not based on anything good we have done or will do, but is solely because of God's good pleasure. And the good news is that we are chosen *in Christ*, the Beloved Son, and through faith in him we are granted the privilege of becoming beloved children of God (cf. Eph. 1:4–6).

This brings us to a very practical question: how do we know whether we are elect? One way is by asking whether we love the things God loves. Do we love Jesus? Do we look to him in faith as our only hope for salvation? Do we seek to honor him and follow his commandments? Do we mourn over and repent of our sins? These are some indications of election. There is no love more precious, no word more reassuring, than to know that God has purposed to choose us in Christ before the foundation of the world—even if the world itself thinks we are no better than scallywags. We may be exiles, but we are *elect* exiles.

Along with the election of God, we also read of his foreknowledge (1 Peter 1:2). God not only foreknows our *situation*—a reminder that all things are in his hands—but also foreknows *his people*. As Edmund Clowney states: "The expression *foreknowledge* does not mean that God had information in advance about Christ, or about his elect. Rather it means that both Christ and his people were the objects of God's loving concern from all eternity"[6] (1:20). This is a deep, loving, personal foreknowledge that should lead us to greater trust and praise of our heavenly Father, who is never taken by surprise.

In addition to the foreknowledge of God the Father, Peter also mentions the work of God the Holy Spirit and God the Son on our behalf (1 Peter 1:2). Here we have an opportunity to reflect on the nature of the indicative of our salvation. The sanctification of the Spirit most likely refers primarily to the work of the Spirit in setting us apart definitively from this world and establishing us in the kingdom of God. The Holy Spirit applies the finished work of Christ to us personally: when we trust in Christ by faith, his blood covers our sins and we become part of God's holy people.

At least two Old Testament passages help us understand the richness of the imagery in 1 Peter 1:2. First is the covenant ceremony in Exodus 24:3–8. In this passage, God sets apart his holy people by the sprinkling of the blood of the covenant, and the people in turn promise to walk in his commands. Again we see that Old Testament imagery for the people of God is applied to the church. But as we read the narratives of the Old Testament, we find that the Israelites failed to keep their end of the covenant. The good news is that God promised to make a new

---

6. Edmund P. Clowney, *The Message of 1 Peter: The Way of the Cross*, BST (Downers Grove, IL: InterVarsity Press, 1988), 33.

covenant, which is established by the blood of Christ (also mentioned in 1 Peter 1:2), and along with this new covenant comes the outpouring of God's Spirit.

This leads us to the second Old Testament text to consider, Ezekiel 36:24–28. In this text, we find that God will overcome the exile and establish his people in their own land. He will sprinkle clean water on them, and they will be clean. What is more, God promises his Spirit to his people to enable them to walk in his ways. Thus, the phrase "sanctification of the Spirit" in 1 Peter 1:2 not only may refer to the once-for-all setting apart of God's people as holy, but may also connote sanctification *by the Spirit* as we are enabled to walk in God's commands. These two aspects are complementary. Now that the Spirit has been freely poured out on all of God's people after Pentecost (Acts 2), we are enabled through the Spirit of Christ to grow more in holiness after the pattern of Christ.[7] Obedience is therefore not something we muster in our own natural strength, but is part of the benefit of being filled with God's Spirit.

We should also note in 1 Peter 1:2 the Trinitarian nature of salvation. Our salvation comes from one God in three persons, each of whom is the same in substance, equal in power and glory. And each person of the Godhead plays a special role in our salvation. In this text we read of the foreknowledge of God, the sanctification of the Holy Spirit, and the sprinkling of the cleansing blood of Jesus Christ. First Peter is an important reminder that the Trinity is not a doctrine that was invented by church councils long after the New Testament, but a truth that is revealed in Scripture itself. And this doctrine is not some theological abstraction with no practical implications; rather, our Trinitarian-shaped salvation empowers God's people to persevere

7. See further Sinclair B. Ferguson, *The Holy Spirit*, Contours of Christian Theology (Downers Grove, IL: InterVarsity Press, 1996), 142–44.

despite unfair allegations and treatment. Let us now consider the blessings of this Trinitarian salvation in more detail.

The Blessings of Salvation

As Peter moves into a reflection on the blessings of salvation, it is striking that he sets it in the context of praise. The blessings of our salvation are incalculably great, and the proper response is to bless God for the riches he has bestowed upon us in Christ. Let us look at a few of these aspects here. Note, first of all, that Peter praises God for causing us to be born again to a living hope. *Born again* is a term that many in our culture associate with a certain type of conservative Christian belief; we may even hear it in association with voting demographics. But according to Jesus, being born again is a necessity for all who desire to be a part of the kingdom of God (John 3:3). In other words, the Bible is clear that a new birth is required, because we are all born into sin and are therefore guilty by nature and by infraction. And the impetus for this new birth, just as we saw in 1 Peter 1:2, is God's own will and action: *God* caused us to be born again to a living hope. Being born again is a gift that underscores the grace of our salvation. Who can take credit for being born?[8] We can also connect the new birth with the forgiving blood of Christ and the sanctification of the Spirit. Indeed, as we saw in Ezekiel 36, the promise of the coming Spirit included the promise of a new heart: an inward change by the definitive action of God that surpassed the blessings of previous generations (see Heb. 10:19–22). Again we see that we are living in the *already* of the kingdom.

Peter adds that we are born again to a *living hope*. This living hope is closely connected to—indeed, it is based on—our living Savior, who has been raised from the dead. Our hope

8. Thomas R. Schreiner, *1, 2 Peter, Jude*, NAC 37 (Nashville: Broadman & Holman, 2003), 61.

is living and abiding—it will never be annulled—because our Savior is the resurrected, exalted Lord of all, and he has secured the benefits of salvation for us. Our hope is also *living* in the sense that it is not futile; it is not based on deception.[9] Our living hope is as sure as the reality that Christ has been raised from the dead. We therefore have a living hope that does not disappoint, but is guaranteed for all time. What is more, this living hope even leads to fullness of life in the present time, as the benefits of the resurrection are already experienced in an anticipatory way by believers now (cf. Eph. 2:6).

But something else is significant about these blessings that we must not miss. God not only bestows on us a glorious salvation, but does so even though we were his enemies (Rom. 5:8). This former enmity is in view when Peter mentions the great mercy of God (1 Peter 1:3). We do not start out in a state of being naturally in God's favor, nor do we even begin in a neutral position. Instead, the Bible is clear that we are by nature enemies of God because of our sin. Yet in spite of the punishment we deserve, God has mercy on us. Not only does he freely forgive the sins of all who trust in Christ, but he bestows blessings beyond compare. It would be impossible to overstate the greatness of God's love for us in this passage.

In 1 Peter 1:4 we see the goal of our hope: "an inheritance that is imperishable, undefiled, and unfading, kept in heaven" for all those who have been born again. This eternal inheritance is part of what our living hope has in view. In the Old Testament, the land and its fullness, with the accompanying blessing of life, was given as an inheritance to Israel as God's firstborn son (Ex. 4:22; Deut. 4:21; we also find that Israel was God's inheritance, Deut. 4:20). We also know, however, that the inheritance of the Promised Land was not the ultimate blessing; it was anticipatory. In the New Testament, this theme is further developed. Jesus

9. Jobes, *1 Peter*, 84.

proclaims that the meek will inherit the earth (Matt. 5:5), and Paul writes that the promise to Abraham was that he would inherit the whole world (Rom. 4:13). This incredible covenantal blessing can also be described in terms of eternal life (Matt. 19:29).[10] As those who are now born into the family of God, we also become those who inherit the blessings promised to God's children.

Peter's teaching that our heavenly inheritance is imperishable, undefiled, and unfading thus accords with Jesus' advice that we should store up for ourselves treasure in heaven, where it is secure (Matt. 6:20). In contrast to worldly goods, our eternal inheritance will never pass away, will never be tarnished, and will never wane in beauty. To speak in modern-day terms, our heavenly inheritance yields an incredible return on investment. What an encouragement this permanence would have been for those exiles who may have left homes, livelihoods, and possibly earthly inheritances behind. What an encouragement this should be for all of us who live as exiles in the present world. The world may not appreciate our heavenly inheritance, but Scripture tells us that followers of Christ are rich beyond all measure.

The permanence of this inheritance should motivate us in the midst of present pressures. Yet not only is it the inheritance that is kept for Christians, but Peter also tells us that Christians themselves are kept through faith as we await the salvation that will be revealed (1 Peter 1:5). Those whom God has foreknown and predestined he guards, and continues to work in, until the day of final salvation. In 1 Peter 1:23 we read that we "have been born again, not of perishable seed but of imperishable, through the living and abiding word of God." Our salvation is eternally secure because God's Word is eternally secure. Our inheritance is imperishable because God's Word is imperishable.

To drive this point home, Peter quotes from a prominent Old Testament passage (Isaiah 40) in 1 Peter 1:24–25. He con-

---

10. See Schreiner, *1, 2 Peter, Jude*, 62–63.

trasts the eternal, effectual nature of God's Word with the transience and hollow authority of human rulers who oppose God's people. Isaiah 40 is a fitting passage for Peter to invoke, because it was addressed to exiles living in a foreign land under Babylonian rule. Isaiah foretold the day when the Lord would break through in history to deliver his people from exile. The situation of Isaiah's audience and the situation of Peter's audience were similar. Peter is assuring his readers that God knows their troubles and would deliver them.[11] Whereas opposition to believers in Christ is fleeting, their eternal inheritance is firmly established.

Peter thus promises that Christians and their inheritance are being preserved for "a salvation ready to be revealed in the last time" (1 Peter 1:5). What is the salvation that is to be revealed? A comparison with 1 Peter 1:7 helps us see that the return of Christ is in view. We will find that the return of Christ is of the utmost importance, both doctrinally and practically, for the early Christians. Perhaps all sorts of things come to mind when we think about the return of Christ—fear, uncertainty, even the particular views of some popular books and movies—but Peter describes the return of Christ in terms of salvation and grace that will be brought to us (1:13; 5:4). Indeed, for the Christian, the return of Christ is something to eagerly anticipate. When Jesus returns, he will deliver us from opposition and usher in the age of perfection. When we understand the backdrop of the exiles in 1 Peter, it is easier to understand the early Christian prayer *Maranatha*—"come (quickly), Lord Jesus" (see 1 Cor. 16:22; Rev. 22:20). We should share in this prayer for the return of Jesus because the future blessings (which we begin to experience now) provide hope for the present.[12]

11. See D. A. Carson, "1 Peter," in *Commentary on the New Testament Use of the Old Testament*, ed. G. K. Beale and D. A. Carson (Grand Rapids: Baker Academic, 2007), 1019–22.

12. See similarly Jobes, *1 Peter*, 88.

Not a People, Now a People

In the book of Exodus, God intervenes in history to rescue his people Israel, his firstborn son, from slavery in Egypt. After bringing plagues on Egypt and leading his people safely through the Red Sea, God establishes his covenant with Israel at Mount Sinai. Before the actual covenant ceremony or the giving of the Ten Commandments, Exodus 19:5-6 provides something of a charter for the nascent nation—a Declaration of Independence of sorts—as God declares Israel to be a kingdom of priests and a holy nation. This text stands in the background of 1 Peter 2:9: "But you are a chosen race, a royal priesthood, a holy nation, a people for his own possession."

We have already noted the love of God for his people in election, a theme that Peter reminds us of here. But now he identifies his readers as a royal priesthood and a holy nation. *Royal priesthood* reflects Israel's status as the people of the great King. The Lord demonstrated his superiority to all other gods in the way he defeated Pharaoh and the Egyptians who opposed him and his people. Israel was also a priesthood, which pointed to their role as mediating the knowledge of God to the peoples around them. This will have significant ramifications for our discussion in the next chapter. As a *holy nation*, God's people were set apart by their covenant with God. They were therefore to reflect the holiness of their King by living according to God's law.

Both Exodus and 1 Peter reflect the indicative-imperative structure that pervades the biblical worldview. Notice that before God gives his law (first in Ex. 20–23), he intervenes to save his people from slavery (Ex. 4–17). Thus, the indicative precedes the imperative already in the Old Testament. Likewise in 1 Peter, Christians are identified as the elect of God that are chosen for God's own possession (indicative). On the basis of this great indicative, we are set apart to be holy, in order that we might proclaim the excellencies of the One who has called us out of darkness into light (1 Peter 2:9). Understanding this structure should greatly help if we are ever tempted to think that either the Old Testament or the New Testament gives us commands to follow in order that we might *earn* salvation. May it never be! Instead, God intervenes to save his people, and his chosen people are consequently to live lives of holiness as a beloved, royal priesthood.

The greatness of this blessing for God's people is magnified when we take into consideration that this high privilege is now applied to those who were outside the general purview of covenant blessings in the Old Testament. Peter is likely addressing mainly Gentiles (that is, non-Jews), those who were formerly not a people (2:10), who had been redeemed from futile ways inherited from their ancestors (1:18). Again we see the great mercy of God in extending the privileges of being his people to all who believe in Christ, even those who may be Gentiles by race.

Since this applies to most who make up the church today, it is worth pausing to reflect on the magnanimous mercy of God to seek those of us who by nature might not be expected to participate in God's blessing, but who have now been brought near because of the scope of God's love. Once we were in darkness, without mercy, and apart from Christ. But now, if we believe in Christ, we are the people of God who receive mercy and walk in his marvelous light. Gentiles are not second-class citizens in the eyes of God; they are not "Plan B." Instead, Peter shows us that the church, composed of both Jew and Gentile, is the people of God and heir to the glorious promises of the Old Testament. Therefore, Peter uses the Old Testament extensively to explain the glories of Christ's work.

Before we continue, we should consider two aspects of how we should understand the Old Testament prophets in relation to our salvation. We will focus here on 1 Peter 1:10–12. First,

Old Testament prophecy is thoroughly about Christ's sufferings and subsequent glories. Peter is not the first to point this out, but is following the explanation given by Jesus himself, who explained the Christological character of Old Testament revelation on the road to Emmaus after his resurrection:

> Then he said to them, "These are my words that I spoke to you while I was still with you, that everything written about me in the Law of Moses and the Prophets and the Psalms must be fulfilled." Then he opened their minds to understand the Scriptures, and said to them, "Thus it is written, that the Christ should suffer and on the third day rise from the dead, and that repentance and forgiveness of sins should be proclaimed in his name to all nations, beginning from Jerusalem." (Luke 24:44–47)

Second, Peter instructs us that the Old Testament prophets were not serving themselves, but were serving those of us who live in the age of fulfillment. Here we might remember Jesus' words that the least in the kingdom of heaven is greater than the greatest prophet of the old era, John the Baptist (Matt. 11:9–13). The prophets were looking forward to the days of fulfillment, to the days when God's true King would rule over all of God's people, and throngs from all over the world would worship the God of Israel. That day is now becoming a reality through Christ, the King of kings.

Returning to Peter's appropriation of Old Testament themes, we find that he utilizes the temple on various levels to describe our salvation in Christ. The temple was immeasurably important for the nation of Israel. Much more than just a place to gather for worship, the temple was in many ways the center of all religious life in Israel. It was the place where sacrifice for sin was made. It was the locus of God's presence with his people. It was understood to be the place where heaven and earth met. If we want a sense of the temple's significance, we might read Solomon's lengthy prayer at the dedication of the temple in 1 Kings 8 (and we might also note the twenty-two thousand oxen and one hundred twenty thousand sheep that were sacrificed on that occasion!). Later, when the exiles returned from Babylon, one of their first desires was to rebuild the temple that had been razed.

In the New Testament we must focus our understanding of the temple through the lens of Jesus. Although Jesus is presented at the temple as a child, and visits the temple on numerous occasions, he also cleanses (or we might even say *curses*) the temple (Mark 11:12–21). Additionally, he predicts the destruction of the temple (Matt. 24:2) and even refers to himself as the Temple that would be raised three days after its destruction (John 2:19–21). Should we then still consider the temple to be important? Indeed, we must. Yet we must also recognize that the temple is more than just a building in Palestine. Jesus has revealed himself to be the true Temple, the reality to which the temple building pointed. He is the One in whom the glory of God dwells bodily (John 1:14). He is the One in whom we trust as our sacrifice for sin. He is the Mediator between heaven and earth. Thus, Jesus' statements show us that the temple is not ultimately a stone building. The temple points us to the person and work of Christ, the true Temple.

This brief survey helps provide the biblical context for what Peter says about the temple. In 1 Peter 2:4, Jesus is identified as a living Stone who was rejected by men but is exceedingly precious to God. This passage has in view not just any old rock, but a living, Temple Stone. In addition to Isaiah 28:16, which mentions Mount Zion, Peter cites Psalm 118:22 to refer to Jesus as the rejected Cornerstone. Jesus quoted from this psalm while he was in the temple during the last days of his earthly ministry, to explain his role as the rejected Messiah who was precious to God (Matt. 21:33–44). Jesus is the living, messianic Cornerstone—the ultimate Temple.

First Peter 2:4 also includes the people of the church as part of the temple in the new era (cf. 1 Cor. 3:16; Eph. 2:20–22). What is true of Jesus is true by extension of Jesus' people, who are united to him by faith. Jesus is the living Stone, the resurrected Messiah who is the locus of God's presence and brings his people in as living stones to be part of the ever-expanding temple of God, mediating God's presence as a royal priesthood to the surrounding world.[13]

We also see that Jesus as the Cornerstone is rejected by men. Yet—and this is hugely significant for Peter's audience—this does not mean that he was rejected by God. On the contrary, Jesus is the exceedingly precious Cornerstone to God, even though the world (and many among his own people) rejected him (Luke 2:34). This perspective provides encouragement for God's people today. Although we may be rejected by the world as scallywags, we are exceedingly precious to God if we trust in Christ. The temple imagery is one way in which Peter communicates this truth.

The rejection of Jesus also highlights the permanence of our hope in a slightly different way. Christ is the Stone of stumbling and Rock of offense: those who revile him will not destroy him, but they will fall. The promise for all who trust in Christ is that they will not be put to shame, since Christ is the immovable Cornerstone that will never be shaken. Like the rock not made by human hands that crushes all opposing kingdoms in Daniel 2:44–45, Christ and his kingdom will abide forever.

Ransomed by the Precious Blood of Christ

As we have already noted, our holiness before God comes through the blood of Christ. Let us now consider three key texts that reveal the nature of Christ's work for us.

13. For more on the temple in Scripture, see G. K. Beale, *The Temple and the Church's Mission: A Biblical Theology of the Dwelling Place of God*, NSBT 17 (Downers Grove, IL: InterVarsity Press, 2004).

First is 1 Peter 1:18–21, where Peter emphasizes the preciousness of Christ's blood to ransom us from sin. We have already seen Peter's concern to communicate God's deep love for his people, and here we see it again. What could be more precious to God than the blood of his own Son? That which Abraham did not have to do (sacrifice his son), God himself did for us. Paul explains the logic of this in Romans 8:32: "He who did not spare his own Son but gave him up for us all, how will he not also with him graciously give us all things?" God has demonstrated his love for us by sending his own Son as the spotless, sacrificial Lamb. Yet we should also not miss Christ's active role in going to the cross: Jesus was not merely a passive victim in his death on our behalf. He was every bit as committed to our salvation as his Father. The persons of the Trinity work together in perfect harmony. Jesus delighted to do his Father's will, submitting even when he was facing the difficulty of the cross. Consider what great love Christ has, to come to us in our humanity and willingly endure the ridicule and shame of rejection for us and for our salvation.

Jesus' death was necessary because he had to *redeem* us. This is a significant term that conveys the reality that we are by nature enslaved to sin. God must intervene to deliver us from the bondage of our own doing, and only the blood of Christ is able to redeem us fully from sin. All the sacrifices from the Old Testament were anticipating his final, perfect sacrifice that no longer needs to be repeated (Heb. 10:14). We should also not miss, however, that Jesus' death is not the end of the story. Jesus' death is effectual because he overcame the penalty of death through his resurrection and ascension into heaven. Indeed, 1 Peter 1:21 reminds us that our hope is in the slain Lamb of God, because he has been raised from the dead and is thus the source of eternal hope.

The imagery of a spotless Lamb slain for his people is also in view in the second text to consider, 1 Peter 2:22–25. Here Peter cites

Isaiah 53, the famous Old Testament passage describing the ministry of the Suffering Servant. We will see in the next chapter how this provides the model for Christians in our own day, but we dare not miss the connection between Jesus as the Suffering Servant and the forgiveness of our sins. Before we move to the imperative, we must take due note of the great indicative of our salvation, that God's Son has come as God's Servant and suffered in our place. He died willingly that he might reconcile us to God. Apart from our trusting in his wounds by faith, we remain slaves to sin. Here we are reminded of the actual suffering of Jesus on our behalf, most acutely as he died on the tree (cross) for our sins. What Jesus accomplished during his earthly life is crucially important; were Jesus' life, death, and resurrection not actual, historical events, then we would still be in our sin. But thanks be to God that Jesus really did come, he really did pay the penalty for our sins, and we really can have eternal life through him. He is the Servant who suffered on behalf of his wayward people.

Before we consider the third text that explains Jesus' work, it is illuminating to observe that Jesus not only is the slain Lamb and Suffering Servant, but is also described in overlapping imagery as the Chief Shepherd (1 Peter 2:25). Thus Jesus is both the Lamb of God who pays the penalty for sin and the Shepherd of the sheep who guides his people and gives his life for his sheep (John 10:14–15).

The third text to consider is 1 Peter 3:18–22, which also combines the suffering of Jesus with his subsequent glory, much as we saw in 1:18–21. The emphasis in 3:18–22, however, is more on the exaltation of Christ than on his suffering. Before we consider this text further, I should point out that this is a confusing and sometimes controversial text, especially verses 19–21. These are important verses and important issues. But it is not my intention to address all the questions that may arise when one reads 1 Peter 3. In my estimation, the main message of 3:18–22 can be easily missed because of the sticky issues that arise in verses 19–21. So for the present discussion I want to focus on verses 18 and 22, passing over the details of 3:19–21. (Interested readers can turn to the appendix for some guidance on how to understand 3:19–21.)

First Peter 3:18 makes several points. First, Christ suffered once for our sins. His sacrifice did not need to be repeated because it was perfect. Second, he suffered in the flesh. The physical suffering of Jesus may seem obvious to us, but it was not always obvious in the early church (nor is it always obvious today) that Jesus really did physically suffer for sins. Third, Jesus is the fully Righteous One, the One who had no sin, and he suffered as a substitute for those who are unrighteous. Jesus was uniquely qualified to suffer for sins because he was the spotless Lamb, the One who was completely free from the blemish of sin. This is true not only because he lived a sinless life of true devotion to God, but also because he was born of a virgin. The manner of his birth guaranteed that he had a true human nature, yet his lack of a physical father meant that Jesus was not implicated in the sin of Adam's race. Fourth, Jesus died to bring us to God. We have already seen how Christ's death brings peace with God, but it is worth noting again because of how fundamental this is to the purpose of the cross. Jesus' death reconciles us to God, and this reconciliation is necessary because our sin puts us naturally at enmity with God.

Fifth—and this is where much of the emphasis lies in this text—Jesus overcame death by being made alive by the Spirit.[14] We thus observe a contrast here between the low estate of Jesus'

---

14. Readers of the ESV will note that I am not following this translation precisely at this point. There is debate about the nuance of the Greek wording here, and the words are flexible enough to be translated different ways. I take the phrase to include a dative of agency ("by") with reference to the (Holy) Spirit. My translation here accords with the NIV (1984), though the more recent NIV (2011) simply reads "in the Spirit." See further Schreiner, *1, 2 Peter, Jude*, 183–84.

humiliation (being made low unto a physical death) and the high estate of Jesus' exaltation (being made alive by the Spirit). From this point Peter mentions some more or less parenthetical details about how this relates to Noah (1 Peter 3:19–21a) and then returns to Jesus' resurrection in 3:21b. The exaltation of Jesus in 3:22 includes his ascension and present reign far above all rulers, powers, and authorities (Eph. 1:20–23); no being in the universe is superior to Jesus. The One who suffered in the flesh for our sins is the One who was made alive by the Holy Spirit and overcame all hostility. The pattern of Jesus shows us how the agony of suffering can lead to glory unimaginable. The call for Christians is to trust in Christ, the ultimate Victor, who will return one day as the conquering Lord of all and deliver his people.

Conclusion

In spite of the trials of living as exiles in this world, 1 Peter encourages God's people with the eternal inheritance that has been secured for us through the work of Christ. Our heavenly reward is sure because God's Word is sure, and because Jesus has overcome all opposition as the reigning King of kings. The reality of the greatness of our salvation is given for our encouragement in the midst of difficulties. Though Jesus is resurrected and rules over all opposition, we must also not miss the pattern of his life: suffering first, then glory. For those who want to experience the fullness of divine blessings, we should not expect that we will receive them in a different way from Jesus himself. In fact, as we will see in the next chapter, the pattern of Jesus' life is the pattern for the Christian's life as well.

Questions for Reflection and Discussion

1. Have you ever been lost or displaced from your home? How did it feel not to know where you were or when you would get home?

2. How was the physical situation of the exiles in 1 Peter related to the spiritual reality of being exiles?

3. What do you think of when you hear the term *election*? What does the use of this term in 1 Peter tell us about God's work in salvation?

4. How might the inheritance that Peter speaks of resonate with the experience of the first audience? How does that inheritance motivate us in the present?

5. Discuss the implications of the following statement: "Our salvation is eternally secure because God's Word is eternally secure."

6. What images come to mind when you think of the return of Christ? What do you think Peter would have us envision?

7. How should the life and ministry of Christ impact our understanding of the temple today?

8. What does Peter emphasize about the nature of Christ's death?

2

SCALLYWAGS TO THE WORLD, BELOVED BY GOD

*Keep your conduct among the Gentiles honorable, so that
when they speak against you as evildoers, they may see
your good deeds and glorify God on the day of visitation.*
(1 Peter 2:12)

*Beloved, do not be surprised at the fiery trial when it
comes upon you to test you, as though something strange
were happening to you.* (1 Peter 4:12)

IN THE LAST CHAPTER we saw that the readers of 1 Peter
are described as exiles, and this depiction provides much of
the framework for how we are to read the letter. Peter's readers
were very likely displaced persons, though the deeper reality
is that all who follow Christ are displaced persons in the present world that often opposes Christ and his people. Living in
the uncertainty of a non-Christian world is difficult, and is
a reality all that Christians can understand (even if we have
not been physically displaced from our homeland).

Thankfully, Peter gives us much encouragement for how we are to keep believing and moving forward in our faith in the midst of hardship. In the previous chapter, we considered some of what Peter has to say about the riches of our salvation. Understanding the greatness of the indicative of what God has done for us is foundational. Building on this, we will now look at what Peter has to say about the imperative—how Christians are to live in light of Christ's work in the midst of a world that will likely resist our faith. The opposition we will face should not be surprising to us, since Christ himself faced resistance and rejection. We will see that Christians are to be concerned not simply with themselves, but also with the good of those around them—even those who might oppose them. The good news, however, is that the glories of the gospel and the promised hope are far greater than any difficulty we might face in the present time. Put simply, Peter insists that following Jesus is worth the cost.

Beloved, Obedient Children

We saw in the previous chapter that we are able to call God our Father, and receive an inheritance, if we have been born again. The Son of God washes away our sin with his precious blood and brings us into the family of God. We are beloved because we are united to Christ, the Beloved, by faith.

We have also observed that the calling of Israel to be a kingdom of priests and a holy nation is now applied to the church (1 Peter 2:9). This calling is also in view in 1 Peter 1:14–16, where Peter refers to his readers as "obedient children" and calls them to be holy as God is holy. In the Old Testament, Israel was known as God's son as early as Exodus 4:22–23. This theme is revisited throughout the Old Testament, but it is foundationally explained in Deuteronomy, which emphasizes God's great love for his people and calls Israel to continued covenantal faithfulness. The numerous references to God's fatherhood and Israel's sonship particularly emphasize God's compassion. We read in Deuteronomy 1:31 of God's paternal care for Israel in the wilderness wanderings, as God carried Israel as a father would carry his son. In Deuteronomy 8:5, Moses reminds the people that God had not abandoned them in their hardships, but that he was disciplining them as a father disciplines his son in order to know their hearts. In the climactic Song of Moses (Deut. 32), the people are chastised for being rebellious children (32:4–6, 18–20), yet at the end of the song we see that the fatherly love of God remains (32:43). The sonship of Israel both reflected God's great love for Israel and called the Israelites to reflect the holy character of their divine Father.

Perhaps the clearest combination of these themes, and one that helpfully illuminates 1 Peter 1:14–16, is Deuteronomy 14:1–2. This section opens with an explicit statement that the Israelites are "sons of the LORD your God," and this is closely related to their call to be holy in verse 2: "For you are a people holy to the LORD your God." In other words, it is because the Israelites are to be holy children, who reflect the character of their holy Father, that they are called to follow the purity regulations of Deuteronomy 14:1–21. This requirement for God's children to be holy is also the presupposition of Jesus, who says that we are to be peacemakers as sons of God (Matt. 5:9) and that we must be perfect as our heavenly Father is perfect (Matt. 5:48). Thus, Peter's reference to Christians as "obedient children" is both to God's inestimable love for his people and to the correlating call to live holy lives. Christians are called to follow the pattern of Christ, who was the fully obedient Son in every way. But far from making the obedience of his people unnecessary, Jesus' obedience as Son of God shows us what it looks like to love God with our whole hearts, and he enables us by the sprinkling of his blood and bestowal of his Spirit to walk in his steps. Peter will say more about Christologically informed discipleship in chapter 2.

Holiness among God's people is incredibly important (Peter mentions it four times in 1 Peter 1:15–16). This holiness is based on God's own character, as Peter shows with his citation of Leviticus 19:2: "You shall be holy, for I am holy." God's Word is perfect and eternal, and is based on his character. Some aspects of Old Testament regulations were temporary and provisional, anticipating and pointing forward to the work of Christ. For example, we no longer offer the sacrifices of the old covenant, because Christ has come as the final, perfect sacrifice; he is the reality to which all other sacrifices pointed (Heb. 10:1–14). But this does not mean that the Old Testament does not still apply to Christians today. Instead, it means that we must exercise wisdom to understand *how* the Old Testament applies to us today in light of the work of Christ. For example, to reinstitute the Day of Atonement (Lev. 16) would actually contradict the later biblical revelation that says that Christ's once-for-all sacrifice is the final, effectual, perfect sacrifice that never needs to be repeated. Before Jesus came, it was necessary to observe the Day of Atonement; now that Christ has come and completed his work, we would dishonor Christ to revert back to the provisional ceremonies.

At the same time, to dismiss all of the Old Testament would be equally egregious. In this case, to ignore the call for God's people to holiness in Leviticus would also be to contradict clear biblical teaching, since Peter states explicitly that the principle of holiness among God's people is an abiding one. Although we might not express that holiness in precisely the same ways as the Israelites were called to in their day (for example, not wearing clothes made from two kinds of material, Lev. 19:19),[1]

1. It is often helpful to differentiate between the moral, civil, and ceremonial aspects of Old Testament law. Although these can overlap, in general we may say that the moral law of the Old Testament abides, whereas the civil and ceremonial had a more temporary function for Israel's life as a nation ruled directly by God. Thus, Leviticus 19:19 is most likely reflective of temporary, ceremo-

the call to holiness based on God's character remains, and this holiness is to be seen in all our conduct (1 Peter 1:15). As part of God's moral law, the call to holiness is not dissolved with Christ and the gospel, but our obligation is much strengthened in a way that sweetly complies with the grace of the gospel. On the one hand, we are not under the law in such a way that we must keep it perfectly to be granted salvation. On the other hand, Christ enables and empowers us to walk in his ways through the Spirit whom he freely pours out.[2]

This means that, in light of the love of God we have seen in 1 Peter, we are also to conduct ourselves with fear during our time of exile (1:17). How can we both love and fear God? The answer may not be too difficult: God is at once our compassionate Father and the One to whom we owe obedience and loyalty. "Our Father in heaven" refers both to God's love (our Father) and to God's power (in heaven). Although if we are clothed in Christ's righteousness we need not fear the final judgment (Rom. 8:1), the New Testament also makes it clear that a future reckoning awaits, and this is part of our motivation for living faithfully in the present age (Rom. 14:12; 1 Cor. 3:8; 2 Cor. 5:10). We need not deny this biblical truth if we believe that we are saved by grace. Most assuredly, we are saved freely by grace alone, yet the obedience that flows from a renewed heart really does matter. (The false dichotomy between grace and obedience is part of what Peter responds to in his second letter.) Moreover, as God's children, we really can please him with our actions, and this should be a significant motivation for our obedience. Likewise,

---

nial laws that reflected the deeper, abiding issue of how God's people are to be holy. Nevertheless, even for these laws we must be concerned with the general equity they require (WCF 19.4). For further reading, see Vern S. Poythress, *The Shadow of Christ in the Law of Moses* (Phillipsburg, NJ: Presbyterian and Reformed, 1991). See also the helpful blog post on WCF 19 by Kevin DeYoung, "A Conversation about the Law," accessed 4 June 2013, http://thegospelcoalition.org/blogs/kevindeyoung/2013/06/04/a-conversation-about-the-law/.

2. I am drawing language here from WCF 19.

our disobedience, while not threatening our union with Christ by faith, can affect our communion with him.[3]

As we seek wisdom for life in this present evil age, we are also reminded that the fear of the Lord is the beginning of wisdom (Prov. 1:7). The relationship between the fear of the Lord and wisdom may also be helpful for understanding 1 Peter 1:17. We are to recognize God as our authority whom we are to follow; his ways are the right ways. In 1 Peter the way of wisdom is not living according to the way of the passions of former ignorance, but walking in the holiness of God's love.

It should be emphasized that Peter is primarily focused on being holy in our day-to-day actions. Peter's exhortation is a very practical one. We are to live holy lives in accord with God's moral law revealed in Scripture. Holiness means loving the things God loves, and turning away from the things that are an affront to God's character. This certainly involves personal purity, but also, as Jesus himself shows us, entails loving God and loving our neighbor as ourselves. In fact, Jesus combines the call to love God from Deuteronomy 6:5 with a passage from Leviticus 19:18 to summarize the entire law of God. In Jesus' day, it was common to identify 613 Old Testament commandments. Jesus boiled these many commandments down to two: love of God and love of neighbor. Thus the call to be holy in all we do is indissolubly intertwined with the call to love God and love others as ourselves. Understanding holiness in this way has significant ramifications for how we live in this world, a topic to which we will return toward the end of this chapter.

Love the Brotherhood

First Peter has much to say about how Christians should relate to the world, but it also has much to say about how Chris-

3. See also Kevin DeYoung, *The Hole in Our Holiness: Filling the Gap between Gospel Passion and the Pursuit of Godliness* (Wheaton, IL: Crossway, 2012), especially 63–77.

tians should relate to one another. Peter even points to this "above all" in 4:8. A fitting place to begin our focus on this theme is 1 Peter 1:22, a text that holds together the indicative and imperative quite clearly. The verse begins: "Having purified your souls by your obedience to the truth." What exactly is this obedience? It most likely refers to the past action of having believed in the gospel, with the present implication of now being set apart to God. In other words, obedience in 1:22 is our belief in the gospel message. It is also clear that the indicative is not all that Peter is concerned with, since he notes that the purpose for our salvation is *for the sake of* a sincere brotherly love. The love of fellow Christians is the *goal* or *purpose* of our having been born again in 1:22. The indicative is foundational for the imperative.

In light of the glories of the eternal inheritance and abiding Word of God we find in 1 Peter 1, it might seem anticlimactic for Peter's main point here to be the love we should have for one another. But what Peter is showing us is the practical relevance of biblical doctrine. The Bible is not interested in giving us irrelevant theological abstractions to discuss while looking down our monocles from lofty ivory towers. Instead, Peter is showing us the rich relevance of the gospel message. When we are redeemed from our former way of life, we are brought into a community that is to reflect the love that Christ has for us. Yet we will still struggle with remaining sin in our lives. We therefore need the transforming power of God's grace in order to learn how better to live together and support one another. All that Peter says about being reconciled to God, and about enjoying the benefits as God's covenant people, is not only about each of us individually. Instead, Peter emphasizes the corporate nature of the covenant people of God, reminding us of the foundational command that Jesus gave his followers: love one another.

Let us consider further the love Peter describes. He does not have in view the self-interested, popular notion of love as that which would satisfy our own selfish desires. *Love* is a verb, something we express toward others as we seek their interests over our own, even if it means disadvantaging ourselves. Love takes work. Love as biblically defined can be difficult and unglamorous.[4] Biblical love is about sacrificing self, not retaliating when wronged, bearing with one another, wishing the best for one another, and applying what Paul lays out so beautifully in 1 Corinthians 13 (a chapter that we do well to apply to all manner of relationships and not relegate only to the occasional wedding ceremony).[5] Indeed, if we want to know what Peter means by *love*, we should reflect on what he has written about Jesus, the Suffering Servant who has given his life for us. We know what love is because Jesus showed us what love is, even while we were still enemies. He suffered not because he deserved it, but because he loves us.

Some nitty-gritty detail on how to love is provided for us in 1 Peter 2:1: we are to "put away all malice and all deceit and hypocrisy and envy and all slander." In 3:8 we are called to have unity of mind, sympathy, humility of mind, and tenderness of heart. Perhaps these instructions seem pedestrian when we have so many big issues to consider as we live the Christian life in today's world, but Jesus teaches us that love is exceptionally important for his followers. The difficult reality is that loving one another is easier said than done. How quickly do we put others down to make ourselves look better? How eager are we to hold grudges and keep a record of wrongs, even against our brothers and sisters in the church? How often do we rejoice with others? Let us put away all competition, backbiting, slander, and hatred in light of the new birth we have received, making every effort to

---

4. Though this definition certainly does not negate the special, privileged, and joyous love of, for example, a husband and a wife. But even in that context, love takes work and is something that we express for the other person's benefit.

5. For an excellent study of 1 Corinthians 13 as it relates to Jesus, see Philip Graham Ryken, *Loving the Way Jesus Loves* (Wheaton, IL: Crossway, 2012).

love one another from a pure heart (3:8). Love covers a multitude of sins (4:8) not because we are unaware of the faults of others, but because we follow the pattern of Christ and choose in love to forgive the sins of others.

We can also relate this to the theme of exiles. Our brothers and sisters in Christ should be singularly precious to us as those who share in our exile. We have the same Father, the same Savior, and the same Spirit, and we look ahead together to a shared hope. Perhaps you have even had the experience, as if happening upon a soft, verdant oasis in an arid and cracked land, of crossing paths with a fellow Christian at a time of great frustration or difficulty, a time when you could almost feel the weight of the world on your shoulders. If you have ever been blessed by the encouragement of a fellow Christian at a time like this, then you know how refreshing it can be. It lifts your spirit. It renews your faith and encourages you to cling anew to Christ and his promises. In light of Peter's exhortations, let us live intentionally and lovingly with one another, considering how we might even stir one another up to love and good deeds, and encouraging one another each day not to have our hearts hardened by the deceitfulness of sin (Heb. 3:13; 10:24). Peter further reminds us that the trials we face are being faced by Christians throughout the world (1 Peter 5:9). Let us encourage one another to keep moving forward by faith, since the end of all things is at hand (4:7).

The Pattern of Jesus: Suffering unto Glory

Among the distinctive features of 1 Peter is the way that Christ's life provides the pattern for the life of the Christian. We see this perhaps most clearly in 1 Peter 2:21–24, where the suffering of Christ is given as the example for us, that we might follow in his steps. As we saw in the previous chapter, there is an emphatic uniqueness to the suffering of Christ. He is the spotless Lamb of God who suffered in the flesh, the righteous for the unrighteous, to bring us to God (3:18). Yet Peter also identifies this pattern of enduring suffering for the sake of future glory as the normal pattern for the Christian life. If Jesus, the beloved Son of God, endured suffering in the flesh, why would we expect to escape suffering when we identify with him as Christians? But there is an incredibly hope-inspiring word here as well: just as surely as Jesus' suffering led to eternal glory, so will those who trust in him by faith experience glory on the other side of suffering. We do not follow in his steps in a way that earns our salvation, but we follow as his sheep. He brings us where he is. As one commentator puts it: "Christ's past and the Christians' present are paralleled, and Christ's present and the Christians' future are similarly paralleled."[6]

Thus, although Jesus suffered in a saving way for our sins, Peter also makes it clear that the pattern of Jesus' life is to be the pattern of our lives as well. This example of Christ is immensely practical for those facing opposition in this world. How exactly are we to follow in his steps? We can see at least three ways in 1 Peter 2:22–23. First, just as Jesus committed no sin, nor was there any deceit in his mouth, we are to be blameless. Of course, I am not saying that we can be like Jesus in complete perfection. By no means! But the pattern of his faithful living is the pattern for us as well. In the midst of difficulty and opposition, he was found to be faultless. Although we cannot be perfectly fault-less, you and I are called to imitate his pattern of life in which he did not kowtow to the temptations of this age. Jesus did not face trials and sufferings because he had done anything wrong, and he did not respond in sin in the midst of the situation. For those of us who may face opposition because of our identification with Christ, a look to our Lord reveals the faithfulness we should demonstrate in the midst of suffering.

6. Paul J. Achtemeier, *1 Peter: A Commentary on First Peter*, Hermeneia (Minneapolis: Fortress, 1996), 68.

Second, and focusing on an aspect of the previous point, we see in 1 Peter 2:22 that part of Jesus' restraint was verbal. When reviled and verbally accosted, Jesus did not retort in anger. For this point, Peter cites the Suffering Servant passage of Isaiah 53, emphasizing the climactic suffering of Jesus' life in his unlawful arrest, sham of a trial, and merciless beating and crucifixion. Even in the midst of the greatest injustice and evil the world had ever known—they were crucifying the Lord of glory! (1 Cor. 2:8)—Jesus did not respond in anger. It can be easy for us to use words in the midst of difficulty to speak in anger against others, perhaps to those who may really be in the wrong. But the pattern of Jesus encourages us not to speak a word of retaliation or vengeance.

This brings us to our third observation from this text. Why could Jesus be content not to retaliate, curse, or revile when reviled? The answer: Jesus trusted his Father, who he knew saw all things and was the righteous Judge; God would make all things right in his time. Understanding that God is in control and that he will judge in his own time gives us confidence not to take our own vengeance, but to leave room for the vengeance of God (Rom. 12:19–21). Let us not usurp the prerogative of God. Instead, let us endure with confident patience the insults and sufferings we may face, always trusting that our heavenly Father sees and will fulfill his promise to vindicate and deliver his people, just as he did his own Son.

These are important points indeed, but we still have not come to Peter's main point in these verses, which comes in 1 Peter 2:24. There are numerous biblical ways to answer the question, "Why did Jesus die for our sins?" For example, we could point to the need for Jesus to bring us to God (1 Peter 3:18), or we could highlight the love of God (John 3:16). That question is answered here, though a slightly different answer is given than what we might expect. I will paraphrase 1 Peter 2:24 to demonstrate the main point: "He himself bore our sins in his body on the tree, *for*

the purpose that we might die to sin and live to righteousness."
In 2:24, the reason given for Jesus' dying for our sin is that we
might live lives of righteousness and holiness.[7] In this context,
"living to righteousness" is not describing the imputation of
Christ's righteousness to us, though that is indeed a biblical
necessity if we are to be acceptable in God's sight. Instead, Peter
explains that the point of Jesus' dying for our sin is that we
might be characterized by righteousness, following the steps of
Jesus himself. Thus, we seem to have again in 2:24 the core of
the indicative-imperative relationship laid out for us. Because
Christ has died for our sins, we are therefore able to live to righteousness; had Christ not died for our sins, we would not be able
to live to righteousness.

Additionally, as we saw in the last chapter, Jesus' suffering did not mean that he was rejected by God or that he had
done anything wrong. Therefore, when Christians face trials,
it does not mean that God has forsaken us. On the contrary,
just as God delighted in his Son when he was rejected by the
world, so God delights in his people who follow in the steps
of his Son. The blessing of this world does not equate to the
blessing of God. In fact, the cursing of this world may actually be a sign of God's covenantal blessing. Furthermore, Jesus
does not ask his people to do anything that he has not already
done. We do not serve an aloof divinity who does not concern
himself with the cares of the world. Instead, the Son of God
himself came to be one of us, experience the difficulties of
this life, and even face injustice and violence that he did not
deserve. The cruelty that we may face does not come close
to the evil that Jesus himself faced. We follow in his steps
because he has already gone before us and overcome every
opposition. He therefore now reigns in glory. And as surely

7. See similarly Thomas R. Schreiner, *1, 2 Peter, Jude*, NAC 37 (Nashville: Broadman
& Holman, 2003), 145.

as Christ reigns, he promises that his people will reign with him (2 Tim. 2:12; Rev. 20:6).

In sum, if Jesus was viewed as a scallywag to the world, the same will be true of his people. But just as Jesus was delivered unto glory, the pattern of his life that led to glory will also be true for Christians because of our connection to Christ by faith.

The Fiery Trial

Even though Christians will face suffering in this world, Peter also emphasizes that Christians must be model citizens. In fact, one of the surprising or disconcerting aspects of the suffering that Christians are called to endure is the fact that it seems so misplaced. Why would Christians be persecuted in the first place? Is it because they really are scallywags who disrupt society? Do they bring it on themselves? Or is there a divine reason for the suffering? We will look at the answers to these questions in this section in relation to what Peter calls the *fiery trial*.

Christians in Public Life

One of the emphases of 1 Peter is the role of Christians in the larger society. From the backlash that Peter is preparing his readers for, you might think that Christians were called to be disturbers of the peace. Not so! Instead, Peter makes it clear that Christians are to be the models of virtue in public and at home, and, like Jeremiah in the Old Testament, are to seek the welfare of the society in which we are exiles (Jer. 29:4–7). How do we do this?

One way is to be subject to every human institution for the sake of Jesus (1 Peter 2:13). We are to be model citizens, not covering up evil but being known for our working of good. In fact, we are to be so characterized by our good deeds that those who oppose us will actually be lacking fodder to use against us (2:15). The rationale for obeying the government is not that the emperor is the ultimate authority, but that Christ is: our ultimate allegiance to Christ means that we should honor all those authorities that have been created by God.[8] We are to live as people who are free, but this is not a freedom to do whatever we want. Instead, it is a freedom to serve God by doing good (2:16). The implication is that God's servants do not live wild, uncontrolled lives, nor do we live according to the rules of the spirit of this age, but we live according to God's ways revealed in his Word.

We may not realize how significant a statement this was in the original context. When Jesus said to give to Caesar the things that are Caesar's, and to give to God the things that are God's, he very likely confounded the categories of his audience. It was inconceivable to many of Jesus' Jewish contemporaries that one could be a good citizen of Rome (the oppressor) and be faithful as part of God's people (the oppressed). These appeared to be mutually exclusive options. In fact, in many ways Rome was presenting an alternative religious explanation of the world with its pantheon of gods and goddesses, the myth of the greatness of the *Pax Romana*, and the emergence of the worship of the emperor. Yet Peter (and Paul, see Rom. 13) follows Jesus in telling Christians to be subject to the government, which is instituted by God to restrain evil and serve the good. Jesus informs us that it is indeed possible to be faithful citizens of the kingdom of God and good citizens in an earthly kingdom, though it will often take a great deal of wisdom.

For example, this call to be model citizens must be balanced with the primary allegiance that Christians have to Jesus. If Christians are ever compelled to turn their backs on Jesus, perhaps commanded to worship the emperor—something that we

8. This is the way in which "every human institution" is described in 1 Peter 2:13. The precise wording is "every human creation" (πάσῃ ἀνθρωπίνῃ κτίσει).

know did happen in the Roman Empire—then Christians must not hesitate to obey God rather than men (Acts 4:19–20), since it is Jesus (not Caesar) who is Lord of all (Acts 10:36). The New Testament also warns us against the unbridled power of ungodly structures. For example, the beast from the sea in Revelation 13 most likely refers to oppressive governments that oppose God's people. Even in 1 Peter we see the assumption that Christians may suffer injustice because of the name of Christ (4:16). Thus we have clear statements that Christians must be model citizens who do good, but if asked to contravene God's Word we must obey God rather than men.

Christians at Home

In addition to being model citizens in public life, Christians seek the welfare of society by the virtue we demonstrate at home. Christians are to be neither scallywags to the public order nor scallywags who bring chaos to the sphere of family life.

We turn now to 1 Peter 3. Here Peter addresses wives first, exhorting them to be subject to their own husbands (3:1). For encouragement in this, if we look just above 3:1 to 1 Peter 2:21–25, we see the example of Jesus, who, though he did no wrong, endured suffering because he was faithful to God. This willingness to submit is not based on inferiority in any way. But just as the eternal Son of God willingly humbled himself for the sake of his people, so Christian wives, as elect and beloved by God, are to humble themselves willingly for the sake of their husbands even if it may be difficult.

It might be difficult, because 1 Peter 3 has in view primarily mixed marriages (spiritually speaking) between Christians and non-Christians (though it will also have application to wives with Christian husbands). In this context Christian wives may have broken with cultural norms by following Christ even if their

43

husbands did not.[9] A situation that was not uncommon in the early church, and a situation that many face today, is the issue of how to live as a Christian in a marriage in which the husband (or wife) does not share the faith of the spouse. This can lead to disharmony and tension. Peter has this sort of marriage particularly in view when he instructs wives to win their husbands (those who do not obey the Word) "without a word" (3:1). Stated simply, it is often wise not to respond with words when reviled or insulted because of one's faith, and in the context of marriage, loving service will be more strategic than many words. As she submits to her husband, even an unbelieving husband, a wife has an opportunity to display the love of Christ in a distinctive way.[10]

The Bible's message on this issue is not irrelevant for our day. Although some might think this text sounds restrictive, in the Greco-Roman world into which 1 Peter was written, the teaching of 1 Peter would have been countercultural. By way of contrast, one well-known non-Christian writer from the ancient world tells husbands to *control* their wives.[11] Additionally, the elite in the Greco-Roman world commonly believed that women were inferior to men: they often believed that women lacked the same capacity to reason, were ruled by their emotions, and tended toward wickedness, greediness, immorality, and contentiousness.[12] This is emphatically not the view of the Bible. The Bible does not command husbands to control their wives, but calls wives willingly to submit to their husbands. Moreover, wives were often not addressed at all in philosophical literature pertaining to household relationships, but Peter addresses wives first.[13] Furthermore, husbands are called to live with their wives

9. See Karen H. Jobes, *1 Peter*, BECNT (Grand Rapids: Baker Academic, 2005), 186.

10. Edmund P. Clowney, *The Message of 1 Peter: The Way of the Cross*, BST (Downers Grove, IL: InterVarsity Press, 1988), 129.

11. See the discussion of Plutarch in ibid., 127.

12. See Achtemeier, *1 Peter*, 206.

13. Jobes, *1 Peter*, 184–86.

in an understanding way, as they *honor* their wives (3:7), which is a distinctively Christian ethic that appears to be unique among Greco-Roman literature.[14] Indeed, this text underscores the necessity that a husband love and honor his wife, lest his prayers be unanswered (3:7).[15]

To place 1 Peter 3 in broader biblical perspective, we see that men and women are both made in the image of God, yet they have different roles in marriage. The husband and wife are to follow the pattern of Christ in distinct ways. The wife is to follow the pattern of Christ by submission, and the husband is to follow the pattern of Christ by honoring his wife and demonstrating self-sacrificial love. Yet a difference in roles within marriage does not entail a difference in dignity.[16] Thus, we see in 1 Peter 3:7 that men and women are coheirs of the grace of life, even though different roles in marriage are described. We find a similar discussion of marriage in Ephesians 5:22–33. As we see throughout the New Testament, wives are called in Ephesians 5 to submit to their husbands. But the call to husbands is even more radical: husbands are to love their wives as Christ loved the church. This is a love unto death, a love that does not seek its own interests but serves the interests of the other person. Marriage is one of the most beautiful pictures that God has given us of the unity of Christ and his church, and it must not be perverted into a pretext for power plays or self-advancement.[17] Marriage should be a brilliant beacon to the world of the radiant love of Jesus Christ, who gave his life for our ultimate good. May God grant us grace in marriage that we might experience this unity and

14. Schreiner, *1, 2 Peter, Jude*, 161.

15. See also ibid.

16. As Schreiner states (ibid., 151): "Those who argue that a different function implies inequality betray a secular worldview that identifies worth with stature and the exercise of authority."

17. It should be emphasized that the Bible does not condone abuse in marriage in any way; cf. Jobes, *1 Peter*, 206.

allow the rays of its beauty to break through from our homes into the world.

If Christians are to be model citizens and embody the love of Christ in our homes, we might expect that the world will have no problems with us. To be sure, Peter does indicate that the government often does protect those who do good. Yet Peter also reminds us not to be surprised when the fiery trial comes upon us. Why would a fiery trial come upon us if we are following our self-sacrificing Savior? A simple answer to this question is that the world was opposed to Christ himself. Thus, we should not be surprised when we face opposition and are labeled scallywags—or worse—by the world, even as we seek the welfare of society. Jesus even warned us that if they called him the devil (much worse than a scallywag!), then the world will also malign his disciples (Matt. 10:25).

So what is the fiery trial that Peter describes? In Peter's day it was probably not the threat of martyrdom, though that did soon become a reality. Instead, it seems to be the social pressures, economic hardships, ridicule, and opposition that God's people face in a world that does not acknowledge him as the true King. Notice what Peter says in 1 Peter 4:3–5:

> For the time that is past suffices for doing what the Gentiles want to do, living in sensuality, passions, drunkenness, orgies, drinking parties, and lawless idolatry. With respect to this they are surprised when you do not join them in the same flood of debauchery, and they malign you; but they will give account to him who is ready to judge the living and the dead.

So because Peter's readers in exile did not live according to the spirit of the age, they were viewed as strange and immoral. Things that were deemed normal by society were understood by Christians to be contrary to the will of God, and were therefore activities that they could not participate in. This lack of conformity to the status quo ruffled feathers, and Christians were often demonized because of it.

Perhaps it is not too difficult to read this passage and think of our own day, particularly given the focus in 1 Peter 4:3–5 on sexual licentiousness. So often today, anyone who believes that sex is to be celebrated only in the context of a marriage between a man and a woman is dismissed as antiquated, uneducated, or perhaps even dangerous. It is unthinkable to many in our society that God has defined the boundaries of sexual expression and that each person is not free to define sexual fulfillment in any way he or she pleases. But this is exactly what Scripture says, and Christians must adhere to the biblical truth and not acquiesce to society's standards. One of the reasons that 1 Peter is so relevant today is that the present state of Western society favors the Greco-Roman culture of Peter's audience in a number of ways. In Peter's day, pluralism was rampant; an "anything goes" sexual avidity was the norm; society and the government were tolerant of many things, except those religions and people that they had decided they did not want to tolerate.[18] In such a society, we must not be surprised at the fiery trial when it comes.

In the midst of the fiery trial, can we know that God has a plan for what is happening? Yes! The good news is that God is actually testing and proving the faith of his people through these trials. The purpose of the testing of our faith is that it might be purified through fire (1 Peter 1:7). In other words, faith that is tested is a genuine faith; faith is perfected in the fires of affliction. Far from being the sign of God's disfavor, the suffering of the Christian actually serves the purpose of refining our faith, that it might result in praise and glory and honor at the revelation

18. It has been observed that tolerance is a "parasitic concept," meaning that it operates within a worldview that views some things as acceptable and other things as not acceptable. Thus, tolerance is true only to a degree that fits within a predefined worldview. See C. Kavin Rowe, *World Upside Down: Reading Acts in the Greco-Roman Age* (Oxford: Oxford University Press, 2009), 166.

of Jesus Christ (1:7). The eternal inheritance is in view even in the midst of the fiery trial.

This point should bring encouragement to us when we find ourselves in a difficult situation because of our faith. Peter's readers were not being persecuted because of their lack of faith, but precisely because of their faithfulness. It would be a grievous distortion of biblical teaching to say that we face trials only because of a lack of faith. In fact, Peter tells us that the trials we face are to ensure that our faith will yield eternal life. Just as Jesus faced opposition from this world because of his faithfulness (not his lack of faith!), Christians who follow in his steps will also face opposition. Thus Peter tells us in 4:16 that we need not be ashamed of suffering as Christians, as if we had done something wrong, or as if our faith were lacking. Instead we are to realize that we are blessed by God as his children, even when the world opposes us.

In this light we should consider one of the most striking statements that Peter makes. In 1 Peter 4:17 we read: "For it is time for judgment to begin at the household of God; and if it begins with us, what will be the outcome for those who do not obey the gospel of God?" This is another statement that should bring us encouragement. Peter seems to mean that already now, the anticipations of the final judgment of God are being felt in this world. Just as we currently experience the blessing of eternal life in a *not yet* sense, so we experience God's judgment in a *not yet* sense. Everyone is faced with the prospect of God's judgment, but Christians need not fear. The fire of judgment is not for condemnation, but is to prove our faith.

We can also relate this judgment to the ministry of Jesus. John the Baptist predicted that Jesus would baptize with the Holy Spirit and with fire (Luke 3:16). Later Jesus connected the fire that he had come to cast on the earth with the baptism of judgment that he was to undergo in his death (Luke 12:49–50).

Thus, Jesus experienced the fire of judgment for his people so that when he does baptize with the Holy Spirit and fire, those cleansed by his blood are not destroyed. We can think here of the tongues of fire that came upon God's people at Pentecost (Acts 2:1–4), fulfilling Luke 3:16. The fire did not harm God's people, but purified and empowered them.[19] Additionally, the Old Testament teaches that God's firelike judgment would first come to the temple (Ezek. 9:6; Mal. 3:1–4), which Peter makes clear is now the church.

Thus, the judgment of God's fire that has already begun is nothing for God's people to fear. The fiery trial may lead to difficulty now, since we live in the tension of experiencing the *not yet* before the fullness of the *already*, but those difficulties will be vindicated because our faith will lead to praise and honor and glory on the final day. "The flames of persecution . . . are a token to Christians of the faithfulness of God who will deliver them from the wrath to come."[20] We should remember that day, and live in light of it, that we might rejoice and be glad when his glory is revealed (1 Peter 4:13).

Glorifying God on the Day of Visitation

As we follow the pattern of Christ and endure the fiery trial, Peter instructs us that we should also think of more than ourselves. Instead, we are to keep our "conduct among the Gentiles honorable, so that when they speak against you as evildoers, they may see your good deeds and glorify God on the day of visitation" (1 Peter 2:12). Christians are to be so saturated with love for those around us as we follow Christ that God might even use us to bring others into the kingdom. In other words, there is a missional aspect to faithful living in 1 Peter.

19. See further Richard B. Gaffin Jr., *Perspectives on Pentecost: New Testament Teaching on the Gifts of the Holy Spirit* (Phillipsburg, NJ: Presbyterian and Reformed, 1979), 14–16.
20. Clowney, *1 Peter*, 195.

God's people have always been called to be a light to those around them. Part of why Israel was to be holy was in order that they would be a witness to other nations of the true God. We see in 1 Peter 2:9 that Israel was a royal *priesthood* and a *holy* nation. The purpose given for this status is *so that* God's people might proclaim the excellencies of the One who called us out of darkness into the glorious light of the gospel. Our goal is not to prove to those around us that we are right, nor to win every argument. Our ultimate goal, as we live according to the pattern of Christ, is that others might see our good deeds and glorify our Father in heaven (Matt. 5:16).

So Christians must have wisdom to know how always to be ready to give a reason for the hope that we have, and we must do this with gentleness and respect (1 Peter 3:15; cf. 1:13; 2:11; 5:8). We may have the right answer, but are we answering in the right way? Our conversations about the teachings of the Bible should be seasoned with equal parts truth and gentleness. The stereotype for many is that Christians are bigoted and intolerant. Yet Christians should be the most courteous and respectful in discussions, even when we disagree with the views of others. We should never call names, label others unfairly, or use incendiary language just because we encounter people who may disagree with biblical teaching. Instead, we should be humble and respectful to all, even those who may firmly hold different views on hot-button issues. Let us speak the truth, but always with love and respect.

As we conclude our reflections on 1 Peter, we should also consider an important motivation for faithful living in the present: the future return of Christ. Jesus is going to return and set things right (1:5, 7, 13; 2:12; 4:5; 5:4; cf. 4:7, 17–18). This also gives a sense of urgency to 1 Peter: this salvation is *ready to be revealed* (1:7).[21] Jesus could return at any moment. Thus,

21. Achtemeier, *1 Peter*, 98.

we are to be thoughtful and watchful, always alert and ready as we anticipate the return of our King. Blessed is the one whom Jesus finds doing his will when he returns (Matt. 24:46). Thus, far from being an esoteric, ethereal doctrine disconnected from life, the return of Christ is viewed by the New Testament as being immensely relevant. When Christ comes again, he will bring vindication for those who trust in him, and he will deal with injustice and lawlessness. For those who trust in Christ, it will be a time of receiving grace (1 Peter 1:13). We should live to please God, enduring suffering when necessary, doing good that others might see our manner of life and trust in Christ, thereby glorifying God on the day of visitation (2:12).

Conclusion

Peter shows us that the life of the Christian must follow the pattern of Christ's life. This pattern moves from suffering unto glory by faith. The self-sacrificial love of Christ and his refusal to wrong when he was wronged must be marks of the Christian. This is the light in which we should understand the familiar exhortation in 1 Peter 5:6–7, which moves from suffering unto glory: "Humble yourselves, therefore, under the mighty hand of God so that at the proper time he may exalt you, casting all your anxieties on him, because he cares for you." Christians can be assured that our future exaltation is as certain as the return of Christ.

Questions for Reflection and Discussion

1. Is the holiness of God's people temporary or permanent? How do we know?
2. Practically, how can we both love and fear God?
3. How would 1 Peter instruct us to relate to those around us who share a faith in Christ?

4. How would 1 Peter instruct us to relate to those around us who do not share a faith in Christ?
5. What is the overarching pattern of Jesus' incarnate life, as it is explained in 1 Peter? What difference does that make for us?
6. Is the fiery trial a good thing or a bad thing? Discuss.

Part 2

SCOFFERS

3

A RIGHTEOUS KINGDOM:
SALVATION IN 2 PETER

His divine power has granted to us all things that pertain to life and godliness, through the knowledge of him who called us to his own glory and excellence, by which he has granted to us his precious and very great promises, so that through them you may become partakers of the divine nature, having escaped from the corruption that is in the world because of sinful desire. (2 Peter 1:3–4)

But according to his promise we are waiting for new heavens and a new earth in which righteousness dwells.
(2 Peter 3:13)

TWENTY YEARS is a long time to be separated from home and family, particularly when the reason for the absence is war in a distant land. These trials provide the context for the adventures of Odysseus, the great warrior of the Trojan War we read about in *The Odyssey*. After a protracted ten-year conflict with Troy, Odysseus and his comrades (most notably Achilles) eventually succeed in bringing down the fortified city through the ruse of the Trojan horse. Yet the end of the war was only the beginning of the difficulties for Odysseus, who faced deadly perils and harrowing travels in his subsequent ten-year return journey to Ithaca, the island kingdom he ruled. King Odysseus was eager to return home, but during the delay of his return, the inhabitants of Ithaca had begun to forget Odysseus. They wooed his wife. They disrespected Odysseus' son and sought his throne for themselves. They lived as if Odysseus were dead. How shocked they were when Odysseus presented himself alive! When Odysseus strung the bow that no one else could, he demonstrated his right to the kingship and put a decisive end to the treacherous intrigues of his rebellious subjects. When Odysseus returned, there was no question that he was the rightful king, and it was futile to oppose this mighty warrior. Ithaca's true king was back.

Although Odysseus had been away for two decades, the citizens of Ithaca were foolish to live as though he would never return. *The Odyssey* is not a Christian story, and we would not want to condone all that Odysseus does in his quest to make it home. Nevertheless, the return of Odysseus to Ithaca can help us appreciate the message of 2 Peter. In his second letter, Peter counters the scoffers who teach and live as if Jesus were never coming back.[1] Thus, they think that they are free to live in ways that do not accord with Jesus' teaching or his kingdom. But Peter urges his audience not to be so easily deceived. The delay of Jesus' return does not mean that he is not in control, and it does not mean that he will not return. In fact, Peter reminds us that the return of Christ is absolutely certain, and that when Jesus returns he will establish his eternal kingdom

1. The authorship of 2 Peter is one of the most widely debated of all New Testament books. Nevertheless, there are good reasons for concluding that Peter was indeed the author of 2 Peter. For a discussion, see Michael J. Kruger, "The Authenticity of 2 Peter," *JETS* 42 (1999): 645–71; D. A. Carson and Douglas J. Moo, *An Introduction to the New Testament*, 2nd ed. (Grand Rapids: Zondervan, 2005), 654–68.

of righteousness. In light of this, Peter exhorts us to live in accord with Jesus' kingship and kingdom now, looking forward to the righteousness that will be fully established when King Jesus appears.

Partakers of the Divine Nature

The Greatness of the Indicative

The first verse of 2 Peter already emphasizes the indicative of our salvation: "To those who have obtained a faith of equal standing with ours *by the righteousness of our God and Savior Jesus Christ.*" We see here that we have obtained (or received) our faith *through* the righteousness of Jesus Christ. Thus our faith comes not from ourselves, but as a result of the saving righteousness of Jesus Christ.[2] Peter emphasizes righteousness throughout 2 Peter, particularly how we are to live in accord with God's righteousness. At the beginning of 2 Peter, however, righteousness seems to refer mainly to the work of Christ for us that we might receive the gift of faith. The first verse of 2 Peter is also significant because it clearly identifies Jesus as God. The New Testament shows us the divinity of Jesus in many ways, but 2 Peter 1:1 is one of the most direct affirmations we find of this truth. Jesus Christ is our God.

As God, Jesus possesses the divine power that grants all things to us concerning life and godliness (2 Peter 1:3). Life here refers to eschatological life—eternal life—that we already begin to experience now by faith in our resurrected Lord. Peter explains that this life entails a conformity to godliness and growth in righteousness. Since Jesus is going to return and establish a perfect kingdom of righteousness, we ought to live in accord with this

2. For an explanation of the rationale, see Thomas R. Schreiner, *1, 2 Peter, Jude*, NAC 37 (Nashville: Broadman & Holman, 2003), 286.

ethic now. Jesus calls us to turn from sin and turn to him by his own glory and excellence (1:3–4).[3] This glorious power of Christ is more beautiful and powerful and wonderful than the world of corruption around us (see 1:16–17). We also see again the divine initiative in our salvation, since it is not we who sought Jesus, but Jesus who called us.[4]

Precious Promises

Peter's second epistle shares with 1 Peter a focus on the importance and power of the Word of God. God always delivers on his promises. Here we see that the promises of Christ are also related to his glory and excellence. Through these powerful promises we are able to escape the corruption that is in the world. What specifically are the promises? Peter may have in mind a variety of promises, but he seems to focus particularly on the promise of Christ's return. For example, we read in 2 Peter that some will question the *promise* of Jesus' coming (3:4), but according to Jesus' *promise* we are awaiting a new heavens and a new earth in which righteousness dwells (3:13; cf. 1:11). Thus, the Lord is not slow in keeping his *promise* (3:9), but he will return when the time is right (cf. 3:8). I will have much more to say about this in due course.

What Does It Mean to Partake of the Divine Nature?

Something else Peter says about the promises is particularly striking. Peter states that the reason we have been given these promises is so that through them we might "become partakers of the divine nature" (2 Peter 1:4). This is a remarkable statement that we must be careful not to misunderstand. Peter is most

---

3. Here I take the Greek datives to be instrumental. See further Richard J. Bauckham, *Jude, 2 Peter*, WBC 50 (Nashville: Thomas Nelson, 1996), 178–79; Schreiner, *1, 2 Peter, Jude*, 293.

4. So Peter H. Davids, *The Letters of 2 Peter and Jude*, PNTC (Grand Rapids: Eerdmans, 2009), 170.

emphatically *not* stating that we become God or a part of God. Fundamental to the biblical worldview is the Creator-creature distinction: the triune God alone is God, and no one or nothing else is God. This Creator-creature distinction will never change. God is perfect, without parts, and cannot be divided.[5] Therefore, he cannot be added to. God is uncreated; we are created. Participating in the divine nature cannot mean that we become a part of God.

Instead, partaking in the divine nature in 2 Peter refers largely to the way that those who believe in Christ reflect God's character as they grow in holiness, sharing in the moral qualities of Christ.[6] We must first be born again into God's family (as Peter mentioned in his previous epistle), and then we will be able to grow more and more into the image and likeness of Christ. As John Calvin says, we partake of the divine nature not in *essence* but in *quality*.[7] Peter is not saying that we can work our way to God, but rather that the saving righteousness of Jesus works in us a righteousness in practice that moves toward the goal of eternal life.

As we see throughout the New Testament, this participation in the divine nature has an *already* and a *not yet* dimension. Already we are brought into the family of God by faith and begin to reflect the character of God through our union with Christ, but we will not be fully perfected until Jesus establishes his eternal kingdom of righteousness. We also see this *already* and *not yet* structure in the corruption in the world because of sinful desire (2 Peter 1:4). Sin in our world has both near (*already*) and far (*not yet*) consequences. In the near sense, sin messes up things right now. In

5. This is known in theological terms as the *simplicity of God*.

6. So Schreiner, *1, 2 Peter, Jude*, 294–95; Gene L. Green, *Jude and 2 Peter*, BECNT (Grand Rapids: Baker Academic, 2008), 186; Davids, *2 Peter and Jude*, 176.

7. John Calvin, *Commentaries on the Catholic Epistles*, in *Calvin's Commentaries*, trans. and ed. John Owen, 22 vols. (Edinburgh: Calvin Translation Society, 1849; repr., Grand Rapids: Baker Book House, 1999), 22:371.

the far sense, it leads ultimately to death and, if not atoned for, ultimate destruction in hell. The good news in 2 Peter is that we can escape the corrupt, ungodly desires of the present age—that which leads inevitably toward death and destruction—through the very great and precious promises of Christ.

The contrast between the life of righteousness and the corruption of the world could not be greater. Christ is pure, holy, true, and good. His righteousness is glorious and leads to eternal life for his people. Sin, however, leads to death and destruction. One of the most important and helpful things to remember about sin is that it is deceptive. Satan is the father of lies, and sin lies to us. Sin promises life and freedom and fulfillment, but it does not deliver on its promises. Sin is the ultimate bait-and-switch. As we will discuss further in the next chapter, that which is contrary to God's law does not bring life. We cannot trick God by defying him and his Word and expect to reap the reward of blessing and fullness of life from it. Paul says something similar in Galatians: "Do not be deceived: God is not mocked, for whatever one sows, that will he also reap. For the one who sows to his own flesh will from the flesh reap corruption, but the one who sows to the Spirit will from the Spirit reap eternal life" (Gal. 6:7–8).

Make Every Effort

The divine promises thus enable us to escape the corruption of the world—that which leads to death—and become partakers of the divine nature, which leads to everlasting life. As we noted above, partaking of the divine nature is preeminently related to the reflection of God's character. This brings us to the list of qualities we find in 2 Peter 1:5–7, qualities that Peter urges us to make every effort to attain. We could easily discuss these qualities in the next chapter, where we will consider some of the practical implications of 2 Peter's theology of salvation, but the close connection between salvation and these qualities makes it prudent to consider 1:5–7 in the present chapter on the indicative in 2 Peter. Indeed, given the close and inseparable relationship between the indicative and imperative in the Bible (though they are distinct), it should not be surprising that Peter moves very quickly from the indicative to the imperative. Although the work of Christ alone saves us, the work of Christ inevitably produces fruit in the lives of his people. On the other hand, we will see with the false teachers that such fruit is not always evident among those who claim to be Christians.[8]

The characteristics given in 2 Peter 1:5–7 (faith, virtue, knowledge, self-control, perseverance, godliness, brotherly affection, love) are all fruits that reveal God's work in our lives. And yet these are also things that Peter tells us to make every effort to attain. In other words, it does not follow that because these are the result of God's work in our lives, we are not called to seek them diligently. In fact, Peter tells us outright to make every effort to seek these qualities. Such effort is thoroughly consistent with the gospel of grace. As one commentator puts it, "God's grace should not lead to moral relaxation but intense effort."[9] The primacy of the indicative protects us from thinking that our natural ability to conjure these qualities will make us acceptable to God. Yet the urgency of the biblical teaching should warn us against disregarding the clear imperative to seek these characteristics.

It is helpful to read 2 Peter 1:8 ("For if these qualities are yours and are increasing, they keep you from being *ineffective* or *unfruitful* in the knowledge of our Lord Jesus Christ") in light of the teaching of Jesus and John the Baptist. Jesus warns against ineffective words that flow from a heart full of evil (Matt. 12:35–36), and both Jesus and John the Baptist agree that God's people must

8. Davids, *2 Peter and Jude*, 186.
9. Schreiner, *1, 2 Peter, Jude*, 304. See also 1 Cor. 15:10.

exhibit fruit of repentance in their lives (Matt. 3:8–10; 7:16–20; John 15:1–2). The goal of entering the eternal kingdom of Christ is held out before us (2 Peter 1:11), and Peter even says that the qualities here are necessary qualities if we are to inherit eternal life.[10]

Thus, the qualities we find in 2 Peter 1:5–7 are fruits that have our ultimate salvation in view. Peter emphasizes twice in this section (1:5, 10) the diligence and zeal we are to have for these fruits because the stakes are so high: "the ethical fruits of Christian faith are objectively necessary for the attainment of final salvation."[11] This is not to say that Peter is teaching salvation by our works. May it never be! He is, however, stating that good works are necessary as the fruits and evidences of a true and lively faith (WCF 16.2). The stakes are high; our diligence through God's grace is imperative. We must always remember that our ability to do good works comes not from ourselves, but from the Spirit of Christ (WCF 16.3).

So one danger is that God's free grace could lead one to think (wrongly) that the fruit of sanctification makes no difference. Peter plainly opposes this view; in 2 Peter 2 he minces no words about the spiritual state of the false teachers who teach such things. A related danger is that we might profess to follow Christ for a time, but then turn away, revealing that we were not truly Christ's to begin with. Our salvation is secure because of Christ's work, but one way we know that we truly have faith in Christ is by growing in Christlike character. Thus, Peter exhorts us to keep growing in godly character, to increasingly exhibit these qualities in our lives so that we may never begin the gradual atrophying of our spiritual lives.[12] To paraphrase the writer of Hebrews, let us consider how we might stir one another up to love and good deeds *today* so that we do not begin to be hardened by the

10. See further Schreiner, *1, 2 Peter, Jude*, 301–5.
11. Bauckham, *Jude, 2 Peter*, 190; cf. Davids, *2 Peter and Jude*, 188.
12. See similarly Schreiner, *1, 2 Peter, Jude*, 305.

deceitfulness of sin. We can do this, Peter tells us, by growing in the qualities laid out in 1:5–7. These qualities are results of God's grace in our lives, yet they are also to be diligently sought after.

Confirm Your Calling and Election

Given the importance of bearing fruit in the Christian's life, Peter further explains our seeking after these Christlike characteristics in terms of confirming our calling and election (2 Peter 1:10). We have already seen God's primacy in our salvation, and we noted in our discussion of 1 Peter that election is an indication that God is at work in us long before we seek him. How then do we confirm our calling and election? In this context it is by growing in righteousness, exhibiting the qualities that manifest the grace of God in our lives.

Before we move on, let us say two more things about this list of virtues in 2 Peter 1:5–7. First, the list is not necessarily sequential. There is no reason why brotherly affection has to follow godliness rather than self-control. Instead, Peter probably intends to give us a literary list of Christian characteristics that are interconnected and, taken together, are indications of and motivations for perpetual growth in the Christian life. Second, it may nevertheless be helpful to note that the list does begin with faith and end in love.[13] Faith is the root, as we see in 1:1, and love is climactic, indicating that love is the ultimate aim of the Christian life.[14] Jesus tells us that the two greatest commands are to love God with all our heart, soul, mind, and strength, and to love our neighbor as ourselves (Matt. 22:37–38). In light of Jesus' teaching on love, Paul tells us that if we have all the gifts of the Spirit but have not love, we are nothing (1 Cor. 13). Let us seek diligently by faith to love our Lord and our neighbors that

13. Bauckham, *Jude, 2 Peter*, 184–88.
14. Green, *Jude and 2 Peter*, 191.

we might continue to grow in conformity to Christ each day, bearing fruit in light of the glory that awaits us.

The Return of Jesus as Salvation

Remembering the Past

We saw in the last section that Peter reminds us of the end goal of eternal life in association with our growth in sanctification. Yet he understands the future in light of past events, and writes to stir up his readers by way of reminder of what they had already been taught (2 Peter 1:12–13; 3:1). To this end he focuses on one event from Jesus' life: the transfiguration (1:16–18; cf. Matt. 17:1–8; Mark 9:2–8; Luke 9:28–36). In the transfiguration, Jesus ascended a very high mountain with Peter, James, and John. While they were on the mountain, the cloud of the divine presence descended and Jesus was found to be talking with two of the greatest Old Testament prophets: Moses and Elijah. Additionally, the appearance of Jesus was transformed (or transfigured) in divine glory, and the voice of God was audible: "This is my beloved Son, with whom I am well pleased" (2 Peter 1:17). As Jesus was heading toward the cross as the suffering Messiah, his true majesty was manifested in the transfiguration, revealing that Jesus, though really a man, was also more than just a man.

What is more, however, is the proleptic (that is, anticipatory) role that the transfiguration plays in relation to Jesus' second coming. The glory of Jesus that was revealed on the Mount of Transfiguration is an anticipation of the glory that Jesus will display when he returns in power (2 Peter 1:16). Put another way, the glory that Jesus displayed in his transfiguration is a guarantee of his return. Peter writes that we can be certain of Jesus' glorious return because Peter himself saw the glory of Jesus revealed, and this is the glory with which Jesus will return in his second coming. The transfiguration was the perfect reminder for Peter to use to help his audience understand that Jesus' powerful second coming is more certain than the next season of the year. Jesus' return is an absolute certainty; tomorrow is not.

Therefore, we must recognize that the return of Jesus is not a myth (2 Peter 1:16). It is not a legend. It is not metaphorical language for a spiritual reality (cf. 2 Thess. 2:2). The return of Jesus will be visible and physical, and every eye will see him (Rev. 1:7; cf. 1 Cor. 15:52; 1 Thess. 4:16). And this return will bring salvation and vindication for all those who trust in Christ as Savior. The flip side of the return of Christ is that it will also be a day of judgment for Christ's enemies. The return of Christ should be something that we firmly believe and something that, as we will see in the next chapter, motivates faithful living in the present age. In contrast, the scoffers deny that Jesus is going to return, and therefore claim that there are no ramifications for deeds done in the body (2 Peter 3:3–4).

Peter wrote to an audience of people who were in a very similar situation to ours today: they had heard that Jesus was going to return, but did they really believe it? Did it affect the way they lived? What about those around them who denied that Jesus' return was going to be an actual, physical reality? Peter responds to this objection by referring his readers to the past. The transfiguration is not an inscrutable episode in the life of Jesus that must remain a curiosity. Instead, the transfiguration provides a glimpse into the true glory of Jesus that will be revealed when he comes again. Just as surely as Peter saw Jesus transfigured on that mountain, Jesus will indeed come again in glory.

The Dawning of the Morning Star

Peter also refers to the return of Christ as the dawning of the morning star in our hearts (2 Peter 1:19). "The morning star" refers to Jesus, known elsewhere as "the bright morning star" (Rev. 22:16).

Jesus is the fulfillment of the prophecy found in Numbers 24:17, the royal star that has come from Jacob and will rule the nations. He is the messianic King who currently reigns and will return to save his people. But if Jesus is going to return visibly and physically, how can he also rise *in our hearts*? The answer most likely has to do with the relationship of the return of Christ and the prophetic Word that is in view. Not only will the reality of the prophetic Word be demonstrated when Jesus returns, but the return of Christ will bring the full revelation and presence of Christ in his consummated kingdom.[15] As Paul says, when the perfect comes, the partial knowledge we have now will be done away with. We will know fully even as we are known fully (1 Cor. 13:8–12). Just as Scripture is a lamp to our feet and a light to our path in the present age (Ps. 119:105), in the future age Jesus himself will shine on our path (Rev. 21:23).

The return of Christ, the bright morning star, will be the final fulfillment of the day of the Lord foretold in the Old Testament (Isa. 13:6–9; Jer. 46:10; Ezek. 13:5; 30:3; Joel 1:15; 2:1–11; 3:14; Amos 5:18–20; Obad. 15; Mal. 4:5). The day of the Lord is the day of salvation for his people, but also the day of judgment for those who oppose him.

The Day of Salvation

Peter thus points to the transfiguration to confirm the truthfulness of God's Word. We must be careful here. It is not as though the Word of God were uncertain apart from the transfiguration. Rather, the transfiguration serves as a corroboratory witness that God's Word—here the Old Testament is probably particularly in view—is and always will be true. Moreover, Peter is primarily interested in driving home the point that the return of Christ— the coming day of the Lord—is absolutely certain, just as the Old

---

15. See Calvin, *Catholic Epistles*, 387–88; Bede, in Gerald Bray, ed., *James, 1–2 Peter, 1–3 John, Jude*, ACCSNT 11 (Downers Grove, IL: InterVarsity Press, 2000), 141.

66

Testament predicted. The Old Testament predicts the second coming of Christ in the sense that it predicts the final victory of the Lord over all his enemies, and the final, complete salvation of his people.[16] The final victory has not yet come to pass. When Jesus came two thousand years ago, he precipitated the judgment, but he did not bring the final judgment against his enemies.[17] Instead, though he did not shrink back from strong words of condemnation (see, for example, the woes of Matt. 23), his first coming brought the opportunity to repent and believe in the gospel. The final judgment will come later, when Jesus returns (John 5:22, 27; Acts 17:31; Rev. 22:12). This second coming is very likely what Peter has in mind when he speaks of the certainty of the prophetic Word in relation to the transfiguration of Jesus. The transfiguration assures us of the glory that Jesus will manifest when he returns to fulfill the prophecies of the final salvation and judgment in conjunction with the day of the Lord, the day that is identified in 2 Peter and elsewhere in the New Testament as the day of Jesus Christ (see, e.g., 2 Peter 3:10, 12; cf. 1 Cor. 1:8; 5:5; 2 Cor. 1:14; Phil. 1:6, 10; 2:1; 2 Tim. 4:8).[18]

Peter's plea, therefore, is not just to believe in the return of Jesus, although that is certainly a major concern of this text. But he has a more overarching point: believe in the Scriptures.[19] The return of Christ is sure because Scripture is absolutely sure. He explains a bit more about this in 2 Peter 1:20–21. Prophecy is true because it does not depend on the person giving the prophecy, but on God's Spirit who is guiding the prophet. When prophets put into words the revelations that had been entrusted to them, they were not simply giving their opinion or fallible interpretation

16. See Herman Bavinck, *Reformed Dogmatics*, vol. 4, *Holy Spirit, Church, and New Creation*, ed. John Bolt, trans. John Vriend (Grand Rapids: Baker Academic, 2008), 654, 692; cf. Justin Martyr, *Dialogue with Trypho* 14.

17. Bavinck, *Reformed Dogmatics*, 4:685.

18. See also Schreiner, *1, 2 Peter, Jude*, 321.

19. See similarly ibid.

of the matter. They were speaking for God himself. Therefore, the words of their prophecies are absolutely certain because they came from God.[20] Thus, the biblical teaching on the day of the Lord and Peter's apostolic words drawing upon the transfiguration were absolutely true, even though the false teachers were denying Christ's return. God's Word remains true despite the scoffers who would doubt God's revelation.

Peter's exhortation is to believe Scripture in spite of the scoffing skeptics whom we might encounter. The truth of Scripture is not an inconsequential or purely academic matter. Believing Scripture is vitally important, because the prophets speak of the coming of the day of the Lord. This will be the day when Christ returns and delivers his people. We are to look forward to the day of the Lord and live in light of it, always being alert, awaiting our salvation that draws near.

We also see here the importance of the *written* Word of God. God's Word remains God's Word when it is written down. Peter refers us to the truthfulness of the written Scriptures (2 Peter 1:20), and he himself writes a letter to stir us up by way of reminder (1:13). Thus, the written Word is to be treasured and trusted. As Calvin states on this passage, "the Lord does not shine on us, except when we take his word as our light."[21]

The Incomparable Majesty of Christ

The return of Jesus and the salvation he will bring also points us to the uniqueness and universal greatness of Christ. Peter himself was an eyewitness of Jesus' majesty (2 Peter 1:16), which is the anticipation of the majesty that will be revealed when Jesus returns. This is the glory of the second person of the Trinity. There is no one else who has existed from all eternity as the divine Son,

20. This interpretation of 2 Peter 1:20–21 largely follows Bauckham, *Jude, 2 Peter,* 229–35. See similarly Calvin, *Catholic Epistles,* 390.
21. Calvin, *Catholic Epistles,* 388.

no one else who came to earth and lived a perfect life, no one else who has died and defeated death by rising again, and no one else who has ascended to the Father's right hand. Jesus now lives and reigns supreme in the heavenly realms with all his spiritual enemies being made a footstool for his feet (Eph. 1:20–23). Jesus has no peer in this regard. There is no other name given among men by which we must be saved (Acts 4:12) because no one else is fully God and fully man, and thus able to atone for our sins as a man and able to raise us to God as the divine Son. Jesus has a greatness that far outshines all created beings in the universe. Jesus created all things and upholds all things by the word of his power (Heb. 1:2). He is the one Judge of the living and the dead, the One to whom all men must give account (Acts 10:42; 2 Cor. 5:10; 2 Tim. 4:1). He is the One who will return to earth physically and visibly, and every eye will see him. The day of visitation will be the end of the world as we know it, when Christ will usher in his righteous and eternal kingdom.

A Righteous Kingdom

Many today are concerned about the end of the world and the threat of imminent destruction. Hollywood makes large-budget movies depicting doomsday scenarios. Since at least the days of the Cold War, the reality that a phone call or the push of a few buttons could trigger a massive chain reaction leading to the swift demise of all civilization has surely made such worst-case scenarios appear to be all too possible. Christians, however, can take comfort in the fact that, whatever man may do, the world remains firmly in God's hands. Indeed, we have in 2 Peter the promise that the return of Christ will bring with it a new heavens and a new earth in which righteousness dwells. Ungodliness, scoffing, and opposition to Christ and his church will be done away with by the cleansing and renewing fire of judgment. Peter uses language of destruction (2 Peter 3:7–12), but the ultimate goal is not destruction but a new heavens and a new earth in which righteousness dwells (2 Peter 3:13; cf. 1:11).

This kingdom of righteousness is the goal that Christians should be looking forward to. Do we long for the day when injustice and oppression will be done away with? Do our stomachs churn at the twistedness we see in the world around us? Do we worry about the world that our children will grow up in? Does it seem as though the sinfulness of society is snowballing down the never-ending hill of destruction? Then let us long for the day of the Lord. On that day, Christ will be honored as the beautiful King that he really is, and he will bring to an end all opposition when he consummates his eternal kingdom.

Furthermore, since we are awaiting a day in which Jesus will usher in his eternal kingdom of righteousness, we ought to live now in accord with that future righteousness. The scoffers whom we will consider in the next chapter claimed that the most glorious way to live is in following one's own sinful desires. But the righteousness, power, and glory of Christ tell us otherwise. The fruit of righteousness is glorious and beautiful, leading to life everlasting.

Conclusion

In Peter's second letter, he stirs his audience up by way of reminder of the things they had been taught. They were not to deviate from the divine message they had received through the prophets and apostles. Instead, they were to pursue godliness and love with diligence, recognizing that growth in faith would keep them from drifting away from Christ. Peter is particularly concerned that they recognize the reality and importance of the return of Christ. As we will see in the next chapter, when someone denies the return of Christ, a number of dangerous implications can follow.

Questions for Reflection and Discussion

1. Imagine that you had lived in Ithaca when Odysseus returned. How would you have felt if you had opposed Odysseus' legacy? How would you feel if you were Odysseus' son? How can this help us live in light of the return of Christ?

2. Why is it not antithetical to the grace of the gospel for Peter to instruct us to make every effort to make our calling and election sure?

3. How does the difficult phrase "participate in the divine nature" provide motivation in day-to-day living?

4. How does Paul's teaching in Galatians 6:7–8 ("whatever one sows, that will he also reap") reflect the teaching of 2 Peter? How does this help us live faithfully as disciples of Jesus?

5. What is the significance of Jesus' transfiguration for how we live today?

4

Scuttling the Scoffers: Implications of Christ's Return in 2 Peter

[Know] this first of all, that scoffers will come in the last days with scoffing, following their own sinful desires.
(2 Peter 3:3)

Take care that you are not carried away with the error of lawless people and lose your own stability. But grow in the grace and knowledge of our Lord and Savior Jesus Christ.
(2 Peter 3:17b–18a)

The Scoffing of Scoffers

The Situation

One of the problems that Peter addresses is false teachers in the church. In fact, 2 Peter 2 contains some of the strongest language in the entire New Testament in order to warn us against the dangers of the scoffers who would lead God's people astray. In 2 Peter 3, we see a specific error espoused by these false teachers that Peter indicates is a grievous mistake: denying the return of Christ.

The warnings of 2 Peter make it clear that the denial of the second coming leads to dangerous consequences. One of the reasons that Peter writes with such urgency before his death is to warn his readers against these scoffers and to remind them of the truthfulness of Christ's return, along with its implications for day-to-day life. We can summarize the false teaching in 2 Peter in two ways: (1) the false teachers denied that Jesus was going to return as the Judge (3:4–9); (2) they taught that we can live in any way we want because what we do does not matter (2:1–22). We will look first at the characteristics of the false teaching (and teachers) in 2 Peter 2, and then consider how this relates to their denial of the return of Christ in 2 Peter 3.

The Sinful Lifestyle of the False Teachers

In 2 Peter 2:1–3, Peter provides an overview of the false teaching. Notice four things from this text. First, the false teachers arise within the context of the church. This is a significant point. In today's terms, this means that false teachers often have *Rev.* or *Dr.* in front of their names. Just because someone is the pastor of a well-known church, or has a popular TV or radio program or a widely visited blog, does not mean that the person cannot be a false teacher. We must test the words and lifestyles of teachers against Scripture.

Second, the words of the false teachers are important. They teach destructive heresies (2 Peter 2:1) and exploit the people with false words (2:3). Statements about God and theology are incredibly significant; fallacious claims can have severe consequences. False teachers lead astray with twisted words that do not accord with the teaching of Scripture. Therefore, we must listen carefully to the teaching we receive, and also be very careful and precise with the wording we use. Theology really matters.

Indeed, notice here that the heresies of the false teachers are *destructive*. Peter will spend much of 2 Peter 2 elaborating on this point. Third, notice that the false teachers not only teach wrongly, but live sinfully. Fourth, Peter insists that the judgment of such false teachers is not idle; it is certain (2:3b).

Two aspects of the sinful lifestyle of the scoffers are emphasized: sexual licentiousness (that is, unrestrained sexual activity) and greed. Peter focuses mostly on sexual licentiousness in 2 Peter 2. These false teachers "count it pleasure to revel in the daytime" (2:13), and they "have eyes full of adultery" (2:14)—that is, they are always on the lookout for women with whom they can commit adultery.[1] They are enticed by sensual passions of the flesh, and they entice others to live the same way (2:18). Peter refers to them as "accursed children" (2:14). This may recall the accusation of God's own people (his children) in Deuteronomy 32:4–6, which would be another indication that the false teachers were insiders among God's covenant people. The scoffers seemed to have taught that because we are saved by grace, we do not have any moral obligations. In other words, they appear to have taught that the indicative of salvation rendered the imperative of obedience unnecessary. In the name of free grace they indulged in sin, perhaps so that "grace might be magnified all the more." This sounds eerily similar to what Paul argues against in Romans 6:1–2. Interestingly, Peter mentions that there are those who twist Paul's letters to their own destruction (2 Peter 3:15–16). Could the false teachers have been distorting Paul's teaching of the freedom we have in Christ as an excuse to engage in sinful activity? This is a strong possibility.[2] In response, Peter underscores that this distortion of freedom was a deadly mistake, one that leads to destruction (2:3b; 3:16).

1. Richard J. Bauckham, *Jude, 2 Peter*, WBC 50 (Nashville: Thomas Nelson, 1996), 266.
2. So J. Gresham Machen, *The New Testament: An Introduction to Its Literature and History* (Edinburgh and Carlisle, PA: Banner of Truth, 1976), 258.

In contrast to the licentiousness of the scoffers, the Bible never makes light of sin, nor does the Bible indicate that continuing in sin is the expected path of the Christian (see further the discussion on 1 John). Paul himself emphatically denies that the free grace we have in Christ should lead to sin (Rom. 6:2–16). Instead, Peter and Paul agree that being freed from sin means being enabled to live for righteousness. Here again let us remember the inseparability of the indicative and imperative. Nothing could be clearer in the New Testament than that our works cannot save us; to think we could work our way to God would be to ignore the problem of sin that can be solved only by the work of Christ. Yet the indicative of Christ's work for us does not render sanctification optional. Those who are saved by the righteousness of Christ will love righteousness and must bear the fruit of righteousness. If we are slaves of our own passions, then we are in bondage to sin, because we are enslaved to whatever overcomes us (2 Peter 2:19; cf. Rom. 6:16–17). This does not mean that Christians will not struggle with sin. The struggle against sin will not go away in this age. But it does mean that sin is not to be the defining characteristic of our lives. The false teachers who elicited illicit sexual activity were not slaves to Christ, but slaves to sin.

This speaks to life in the twenty-first century. Certainly the false teachers in 2 Peter seem to be extreme examples, but it is not difficult to find those today who say that since Christ saves us by his work alone, we are therefore free from the obligation of obedience. This may seem like a valid conclusion if we are relying on our own logic, but Scripture explicitly contradicts this conclusion. Therefore, we must not be fooled. We do not necessarily undermine the indicative of salvation if we teach that the imperative of our discipleship is nonnegotiable. Peter teaches that both the indicative and the imperative are necessary. Indeed, the indicative is confirmed by our growth in grace—the indicative sets us free from sin so that the bondage is really broken. Sin is not the master of the Christian because Christ is more powerful than sin and he has really set us free from sin. Second Peter warns against the teaching that the obedience of those saved by free grace is optional.

Peter warns that the false teachers not only have eyes full of adultery, but also have hearts trained *in greed* (2 Peter 2:14). In contrast to their disciples, who do not have a firm foundation and are being led astray, the false teachers are stable in their greed.[3] The love of money is an ever-present danger for religious leaders, yet it is a destructive appetite. Greediness is graphically portrayed in the Old Testament example of the prophet Elisha's assistant Gehazi, who was struck with leprosy after greedily lying to Naaman in order that he might reap the payment that Elisha refused (2 Kings 5). Additionally, Jesus rebuked the Pharisees for being lovers of money rather than lovers of God (Luke 16:14), and Judas Iscariot was motivated by 30 pieces of silver when he betrayed Jesus (Matt. 26:15).

The love of money is tantamount to the love of self; those who love money do not want to part with their money. Instead, they love money that they might spend it on their own indulgences or securities. The love of money is antithetical to the love of people. When someone gains money for his own advantage to the disadvantage of others, is this the love that is to characterize Christians, especially Christian leaders? Yet this love for money is a charge against the false teachers in 2 Peter. Instead, the mandate is for those with means to care for those without means (James 2:1–9; 1 John 3:17). We should therefore be wary of leaders in the church who are greatly skilled in making money and amassing for themselves material goods. Enthusiasm for self-indulgence is one of the characteristics of false teachers in 2 Peter.

3. See similarly Bauckham, *Jude, 2 Peter*, 267.

Along with the sexual licentiousness and greed of the false teachers, we find their denial of God's authority (2 Peter 2:10). How do they deny God's authority? They do so by denying, despising, or ignoring God's Word. But it is not possible to love God and laugh off his authority over our lives, which comes primarily through his Word. God's Word is personal. It reveals his character. Therefore, to disparage God's Word is to disparage God himself. Thus we even read that the false teachers were denying the Master who bought them (2:1). The false teachers probably did not deny an identification with Christ; they would have described themselves as followers of Jesus. This in itself is noteworthy: false teachers in the church will likely claim the name of Christ, invoke biblical language, and not call themselves false teachers. Yet Peter tells us that all those who deny the Word of God are denying Christ. By referring to Christ as the One who bought the false teachers, Peter is again emphasizing the internal nature of the conflict—those who were leading the people astray would have said that Christ was their Savior. But the stark reality was that their lifestyle, which stood in clear contradiction to the teaching of Christ, was a denial of the Master himself.

The ten-dollar word for this disparagement of God's law is *antinomianism*. Antinomianism is an error that teaches that God's law has no abiding significance for the Christian.[4] Although it is true that the era of the law as a governing principle is over because it has been fulfilled in Christ (Rom. 10:4; Gal. 3:19, 23–24), this is not the same thing as saying that God's law has no relevance for Christians. The false teachers in 2 Peter were wrong to think they could follow Christ while shirking the law of God. Instead, we must understand that the law continues to reveal God's character and that the law continues to provide a guide for righteousness.

4. For a more extensive and nuanced treatment, see Mark Jones, *Antinomianism: Reformed Theology's Unwelcome Guest?* (Phillipsburg, NJ: P&R Publishing, 2013).

Thus, we must not only recognize the indicative of Christ's work for us (we do not save ourselves by obedience to the law), but also recognize that Jesus' teaching stands in full accord with God's law. The law remains a guiding principle for the holiness of God's people today (the imperative). We should be suspicious of those who live like the false teachers in 2 Peter 2, those whose mantra might be: "Free from the law, O blessed condition; I can sin as I please and still have remission." This is not a biblical perspective.

The Denial of Christ's Return

In 2 Peter 3, we learn more about the theological system of the false teachers. Here we read that they scoff at the notion that Christ will return, thereby also denying any future reckoning or judgment. In the last chapter we considered some of the texts where Peter emphasized the second coming of Christ in connection with the reality of the transfiguration. When Christ returns, he will usher in an eternal kingdom of righteousness. He will do away with all unrighteousness and judge the living and the dead. A denial of the second coming of Christ leads to errors such as we find in 2 Peter 2. The false teachers apparently did not believe that God was really going to intervene in our world. Yet Peter teaches that Christ has not yet returned, not because God has forgotten us or is too slow, but because God is patient with us (3:9). He is mercifully granting us further time for repentance. In their error, however, the false teachers denied that Jesus would return, and therefore they denied that there is any need for obedience or conformity to God's revealed will in Scripture. As we will discuss below, the false teachers' denial of Christ's return led to serious errors in practice.

Peter describes for us two diverging options. One way is represented by the false teachers. They followed their own sensuality (2 Peter 2:2) and greedy impulses (2:15), denying the return of Christ and blaspheming the truth of the gospel. The other path

79

we can follow is the apostolic teaching. Peter assures us that he and the other apostles were not following cleverly devised myths or falsehoods, but that they conveyed to us the very words of God (1:16). The way of the apostles leads to entrance into the eternal kingdom of righteousness; the way of the false teachers leads to destruction.

Dangers of Scoffing

Danger of Destruction

As we have noted, the false teaching that Peter is counteracting in 2 Peter is not merely an academic affair. It matters greatly. Those who follow the false teachers are in danger of heading down the path of destruction. The false teachers denied any repercussions for their wayward lifestyles. They were ill-informed of the reality that Peter teaches: sin brings judgment and destruction. This would be a good place to remind ourselves of the deceitfulness of sin: sin promises life and blessing, but it lies to us. Instead, sin brings death and destruction. In fact, Peter indicates that the destruction of the false teachers is sure, and that it will come quickly (2:1–3).

In 2 Peter 2:3 we read that the destruction of the false teachers is certain from long ago. This reference to the past connects the situation of the false teachers in Peter's days with four striking examples of destruction due to sin from the Old Testament era. These examples show us that "God's future judgment of the wicked is certain (v. 3b) because God has consistently judged the wicked throughout history."[5] Peter also points out that false teachers (or false prophets) have always been a problem among God's people (2:1). The examples he gives from the Old Testament era collectively indicate the dangers of disobedience to God's

5. Thomas R. Schreiner, *1, 2 Peter, Jude*, NAC 37 (Nashville: Broadman & Holman, 2003), 334.

Word and the perpetual presence of false prophets. Indeed, these two dangers are often related: false teachers bring with them sensuality that would lead others astray (2:1–2).

Old Testament Examples of Destruction

The first example that Peter points to is the sin of the angels (2 Peter 2:4). This is probably the most difficult example for us to understand today, though it may have been more familiar to Peter's readers. One of the most prominent interpretations of 2 Peter 2 looks to Genesis 6:1–4 as the background:

> When man began to multiply on the face of the land and daughters were born to them, the sons of God saw that the daughters of man were attractive. And they took as their wives any they chose. . . . The Nephilim were on the earth in those days, and also afterward, when the sons of God came in to the daughters of man and they bore children to them. These were the mighty men who were of old, the men of renown.

This passage raises a number of questions, including the identity of the "sons of God." Does this term refer to a group of human beings, or could it refer to angels? Most scholars today identify the angels in 2 Peter 2:4 (and Jude 6) with the "sons of God" in Genesis 6.[6] This interpretation picks up on a well-known story that circulated in the ancient world in which a group of angels (sometimes called *Watchers*) transgressed the boundary between angelic beings and human beings and entered into sexual relationships with women. This supposedly led to the bearing of children who were remarkable physical specimens (the Nephilim), and it also led to the violence and increasing sinfulness on

6. See the discussions in D. A. Carson, "2 Peter," in *Commentary on the New Testament Use of the Old Testament*, ed. G. K. Beale and D. A. Carson (Grand Rapids: Baker Academic, 2007), 1048–51; Bauckham, *Jude, 2 Peter*, 51; Peter H. Davids, *The Letters of 2 Peter and Jude*, PNTC (Grand Rapids: Eerdmans, 2009), 49; Schreiner, *1, 2 Peter, Jude*, 450–51.

earth that led to the judgment of the catastrophic flood of Noah's day.

But another (and perhaps better) option interprets the "sons of God" in Genesis 6 as a group of people, such as the offspring of Seth or earthly kings—either of these groups might be called "sons of God."[7] Indeed, even though many understand Genesis 6 to teach that a group of angels had sexual relations with women, this interpretation faces some challenges in light of other biblical passages. Scripture consistently identifies angels as spirits (Eph. 6:12; Heb. 1:14; cf. Col. 1:16),[8] and we have no clear scriptural text to indicate that angels have ever copulated with human women and produced offspring (or are capable of doing so). Moreover, Jesus states that in the resurrection we will neither marry nor be given in marriage, but will be like angels in heaven (Matt. 22:30; Mark 12:25).

Therefore, we should give pause before interpreting Genesis 6 as referring to marriages or sexual relations between angels and human women. Scripture gives very little information about the sin of the angels, and Peter's focus is not on the nature of the sin, but on the inevitability of judgment.[9] (Additional descriptions of the angelic sin are found in nonbiblical texts, but these accounts are often far-fetched and should not be viewed as authoritative.) Thus, we can be confident, based on 2 Peter (and Jude), that some sort of angelic sin likely occurred before the flood, and Peter uses this example to warn his audience. The angels' transgression of God's authority led not to freedom, but to bondage in gloomy darkness and certain destruction. If not even angels were spared

7. See also Meredith G. Kline, "Divine Kingship and Genesis 6:1–4," *WTJ* 24 (1962): 187–204.

8. See Herman Bavinck, *Reformed Dogmatics*, vol. 3, *Sin and Salvation in Christ*, ed. John Bolt, trans. John Vriend (Grand Rapids: Baker Academic, 2006), 454–60; Simon J. Kistemaker, *Exposition of the Epistles of Peter and the Epistle of Jude*, NTC (Grand Rapids: Baker Book House, 1987), 377–88. Carson also expresses reservations. "2 Peter," 1049.

9. Carson, "2 Peter," 1051.

because of their sin, what will become of the false teachers who transgress God's Word? What is more, the current bondage of the angels is the precursor to the future destruction that awaits them. Thus, in relation to the false teachers, Peter's exhortation is that it is exceedingly dangerous to disregard the teaching of Scripture and call good what God has deemed evil. Despite this warning, the false teachers appear to be blissfully unconcerned about what the Bible says will be the end result of their heresies.

The second example of destruction on account of sin is the generation of Noah's day. Here the point is rather straightforward: destruction came on the ungodly because of their rebellion against God. Genesis 6:5 indicates that the wickedness was great on the earth, and that every thought of the heart of man was only evil all the time. Violence was rampant (6:11), and all flesh was corrupt before God (6:12). This destruction was swift, final, and universal. In 2 Peter, the flood of Noah's day serves as a foreshadowing of the final destruction that will come on those who reject Christ (2 Peter 3:5–7). The good news is that all those who trust in God for salvation are delivered. God did not wipe out all humanity, but saved a remnant (Noah and his family), who became the progenitors of the human race down to the present. God takes sin seriously, but is also rich in mercy and is both willing and strong enough to save.

The third example is Sodom and Gomorrah, cities that were filled with unrestrained sexual sin that was, in many respects, similar to that of the false teachers (2 Peter 2:7; cf. 2:2, 18). We will read more about the sin of these cities in Jude, but let us note here that their sins were not overlooked, but were punished swiftly and fiercely. The destruction of Sodom and Gomorrah is not an irrelevant curiosity of the ancient past, but a demonstration of the ferocity of God's judgment against unbridled rebellion, prominently here expressed in sexual licentiousness. Although

Sodom and Gomorrah are superlative examples of sinfulness (and we must take the warning of their destruction seriously), the reality is that every person born since Adam is in need of God's mercy because of our sin. The incomparable good news is that the last Adam, Jesus Christ, came and lived a fully pleasing life to God, and offered himself as the curse in our place. By trusting in him, we are freed from the wrath of God against sin that we all deserve (Rom. 5:9; Eph. 2:3–5).

We should also note that the ungodliness of Sodom and Gomorrah led to the tormenting of righteous Lot, who was forced to live in a context where unrighteousness reigned. Lot's distress is another indication that sin leads not to freedom and life, but to difficulty, cursing, and destruction. Again, however, we read that God not only knows how to punish the ungodly, "especially those who indulge in the lust of defiling passion and despise authority" (2 Peter 2:10), but also knows how to rescue the godly from their trials (2:9).

A fourth example relates to the pagan prophet Balaam, who was summoned by King Balak of Moab to curse God's people (Num. 22:1–7). Balaam is an interesting character because he ended up prophesying positively about Israel. Indeed, the reference in Numbers 24:17 in the last chapter about the star that will come from Jacob is actually a (true) statement made by the pagan prophet Balaam. Thus, it might seem as though Balaam were a positive character in the biblical story. Yet Scripture goes on to tell us that Balaam himself was not on God's side and would have cursed Israel unless God had intervened (Deut. 23:3–6; Josh. 24:9–10; Neh. 13:1–2). Later, Balaam was destroyed for his role as a false teacher (Num. 31; Josh. 13:22). Balaam not only was interested in money (Num. 22:15–21; 2 Peter 2:15), but also led the people astray to worship other gods, provoking them to sexual immorality, most notably at Baal-Peor (Num. 31:8, 16; cf. 25:1–9; Rev. 2:14). Thus, Balaam is like the false teachers in

2 Peter in three ways: (1) he was greedy; (2) he led God's people into sexual immorality; (3) he was met with swift destruction. In fact, although Balaam spoke the truth about God's people (because God made it so), he was so foolish that he had to be rebuked by his own donkey!

Peter gives us these four Old Testament examples of destruction that followed the sorts of sins promoted by the false teachers. These examples serve as a serious warning against following those who despise God's Word, because their destruction is sure (2 Peter 2:3). God has consistently proved that rebellion against him will be punished. It may seem at times as though God overlooks sin, but he does not. Our only hope for escaping the wrath of God is to trust in Christ as our substitute who bore the penalty of our sin and grants us his righteous status before God. But we dare not call him "Lord, Lord" and despise his Word to us (Luke 6:46). The false teachers claimed to be disciples of Christ, but their teaching and lives (which opposed the Word of Christ) revealed otherwise. The false teachers were promoting that which God opposes. How foolish it would be to follow them! God has much experience in bringing destruction upon those who delight in wickedness. Let us instead be numbered among those who put their trust in God, obeying his Word by faith and enjoying his protection from the destruction of sin (2 Peter 2:10).

We dare not neglect to focus on the good news here as well. Sin can leave us feeling condemned and accused, even if we truly trust in Christ and are following him. But Peter is not speaking of the destruction of those who truly follow Christ. In fact, he speaks in glowing terms of the salvation we have received by God's grace and the glorious inheritance that is prepared for us. Peter is, however, warning those in the church of presuming upon the grace of God and twisting it into an excuse to live however they want. This is not a fruit of grace. Grace produces a desire to follow Christ and a love for the things he loves. It may be encouraging to know, however, that the fruit of righteousness may sometimes be subtle. Indeed, at times the fruit may be as simple as not wanting to sin as much as we do, and desiring to manifest the fruit of righteousness more. There is no reason to think that the false teachers in 2 Peter had any desire for holiness or godliness; they cared only about what they could get for themselves. When we are discouraged by sin, the good news is that God never turns away those who truly turn to him in genuine faith and repentance. We should take great comfort in the tender love Christ has for his wounded sheep (John 10:10–16). False teachers, in contrast, are wolves in sheep's clothing who do not care for the flock.

We should also learn from 2 Peter that false teachers will always be among us (2:1), just as they were around in the Old Testament and just as they were around in Peter's day. Let us therefore be on our guard, watching our own beliefs and encouraging our brothers and sisters in the faith. The false teachers ignored the clear teaching of the Old Testament that shows the consistency of God's response against willful rebellion. They seemed to have been telling everyone not to worry about the consequences of sin, because everything was going along just fine and always would.[10] In fact, however, judgment against sin could come at any time.

It is also striking that at least three of these examples from the Old Testament emphasize sexual sin. This is immensely relevant for those of us who live at a time when the world's sexual ethic is in many ways the driving spirit of the age. God's design for the expression of human sexuality is in the context of the lifelong commitment of marriage between a man and a woman, and the Bible is clear that the willful and flagrant transgression of God's standards leads to destruction. Let us therefore lovingly and

10. Bauckham, *Jude, 2 Peter,* 238.

humbly walk in the path of God's light (cf. 2 Peter 1:19), inviting others to do the same.

Blaspheming the Way of Righteousness

The danger of false teachers is real. I mentioned earlier that the language in 2 Peter 2 is some of the strongest language in the New Testament. Peter here describes those who know the way of truth, but who have turned aside from it. We read that their condemnation and destruction are absolutely certain (2:3). We read more about their profligate state in 2:10–22. False teachers are ignorant of the glorious beings they blaspheme. They are like foolish and irrational animals, blemishes who delight in evil. They are never satisfied with their sin. Instead of being trained in godliness, they are trained in greediness. They are waterless springs who are being prepared for the utter darkness. They offer bondage to corruption and call it freedom. It is therefore no wonder that Peter that says their last state is worse than their first. They are like dogs who return to their own vomit, or dirty pigs that have been washed, only to return to their previous filth. As one commentator puts it: "To sin in ignorance, as the heathen do, is one thing; to sin deliberately when 'the way of righteousness' (2:21) is known and to spurn the gift of righteousness is far more culpable."[11]

Notice also that living in unrighteousness is inconsistent with the gospel, because the gospel is described (here and elsewhere) as the *way* of righteousness and a *holy* commandment (2 Peter 2:21). In other words, the gospel call is not just to believe in our heads, but also to follow Christ in our lives. The grace of the gospel must go hand in hand with a lifestyle of righteousness. The false teachers wanted to follow Christ and also live like the pagan world around them, but this does not align with

11. Ibid., 278.

the gospel call. Worshiping God and indulging in the sexual practices of the world's value system are mutually exclusive. Grace empowers us to live unto righteousness; grace does not give us a free pass to sin as much as we please without care for any repercussions.

Eschatology and Ethics

The false teachers in 2 Peter were clearly in error, and one of the reasons they had veered so far from the way of righteousness was that they denied that Jesus was going to return. In 2 Peter we see with great clarity that eschatology and ethics are closely related. Put differently, how we live (ethics) is greatly influenced by where we think the world is headed (eschatology). The false teachers thought the world was, basically, headed nowhere. They thought things would continue as they were and as (they thought) they had always been. They opined that we should not look for God to intervene in our world, nor should we expect any reward or punishment for the way we live. They neglected to realize that everything had been going along just fine in the eyes of the world in Noah's day until God intervened and brought about swift destruction. Peter is adamant that Jesus is going to return and that our deeds really do matter, even though we are saved by the righteousness of Christ alone.

So where is the world going? Peter explains that we are anticipating a new heavens and a new earth where righteousness dwells, and that this expectation should motivate us to live righteously in the present age. Paul says something very similar in Titus 2:11–14:

> For the grace of God has appeared, bringing salvation for all people, training us to renounce ungodliness and worldly passions, and to live self-controlled, upright, and godly lives in the present age, waiting for our blessed hope, the appearing of the glory of our great God and Savior Jesus Christ, who gave

himself for us to redeem us from all lawlessness and to purify
for himself a people for his own possession who are zealous
for good works.

God's free grace of salvation is for the purpose that we would
be purified and be zealous for good works.

As Peter comes to the end of his letter, he reminds his audience that the day of the Lord will come like a thief (2 Peter 3:10).
It will come quickly, and Peter calls us to be prepared and not
be surprised when it comes. The latter part of 3:10, however, is a
bit more difficult to understand. Is Peter describing the destruction of the earth or the renewal of the earth? The overall point
seems to be that the world as we know it will be done away with.
This will involve a purging fire of cleansing—fire that will (like
the water in Noah's day) cleanse the world of the impurity of
ungodliness for the sake of righteousness. Peter seems to be
describing the great conflagration at the end of time in which
the deeds of humanity are laid bare before God's testing fire of
judgment (cf. 1 Cor. 3:13).[12] The heavens will be pulled away, the
intervening heavenly bodies (and/or the materials that compose
our present world) will be dissolved with fire, and all the works
of humanity on the earth will be "found" (in the sense of being
in full view of God). There will be nothing to hide behind. The
day of the Lord will expose human deeds to judgment. And just
as the flood in Noah's day led to a new creation (2 Peter 3:5), the
purifying fire of God will lead to a new heavens and a new earth
in which righteousness dwells (3:13).

Thus Peter underscores the importance of Christian obedience. The Bible does teach that our deeds are important for
the day of judgment, even for those who are saved by the righteousness of Christ alone. This is a tricky topic to navigate, but
we must affirm at least two things: (1) Justification is God's free

12. See ibid., 319.

gift to us, and we will never be justified before God on the basis of what we have done (Eph. 2:8–9). (2) Our obedience that flows from faith is vitally important (1 Cor. 3:8–14; 2 Cor. 5:10). God in his divine wisdom will take into account our deeds, and we will be rewarded according to what we have done (see, e.g., Matt. 5:12; 6:1, 20; Luke 6:23). This teaching need not be confused with works-righteousness, since we know that our righteous standing before God comes from outside ourselves, not from what we can do. This teaching should, however, warn us against saying that what we do is of no consequence. On the contrary, we see throughout 1–2 Peter that obedience matters a great deal. It is dangerous and unbiblical to say otherwise. Let us not follow the error of thinking that sin is just as pleasing to God as obedience.

The importance of understanding rightly the return of Christ also underscores the dangerous ramifications that false teaching has for everyday life. To deny the return of Christ and the future judgment can lead to an attitude that denies responsibility for our actions. To say that we are not accountable to God is to remove an important safeguard against sin and motivation to obedience that God has given us (WCF 33.3). The return of Christ should encourage us in the present age as we live in anticipation of the eschatological realization of God's kingdom in the future.

The eschatology pertaining to the end of the world that Peter gives us is therefore for the purpose of leading us to lives of greater godliness and holiness (2 Peter 3:11). The Bible does not give us insight about the future so that we can speculate with charts and timelines. Instead, Scripture teaches that no one knows when Jesus will return (Matt. 24:36; Mark 13:32). This mystery should encourage us to live faithfully in the present age, since he could return at any moment.

In fact, Peter also says something remarkable here about the obedience of God's people: living godly lives characterized by repentance may actually *hasten* the day of the Lord (2 Peter 3:12).

We have read, for example, that the reason for Christ's tarrying before his second coming is the grace of God, giving us time for repentance (3:9). From a human standpoint, repentance and holy living may hasten Christ's return. Nevertheless, our responsibility "does not detract from God's sovereignty in determining the time of the End . . . but means only that his sovereign determination graciously takes human affairs into account."[13] Let us not despise God's mercy, but take each moment as a gracious opportunity to repent and walk in the way of righteousness.

Conclusion

Peter had to counter the teaching of the scoffers, who were more interested in money and sex than with the care of God's people and the reality of Christ's return. We face the same temptations today. Will we listen to the spirit of this age and assume that things will "keep on keeping on" as they are, or will we trust in the Scriptures that teach the reality of Jesus' majesty and his imminent return? What we believe about where the world is heading will make all the difference in how we live. The delay in Christ's return is an indication of the rich mercy of God, who is giving us more time to repent. Let us take him up on his offer and turn eagerly to our Savior, who would save us from the coming punishment against sin. Indeed, the return of Christ should not only deter us from sin, but also give us consolation in adversity.

Questions for Reflection and Discussion

1. What are some of the characteristics of the scoffers in 2 Peter?
2. Why are false teachers sometimes described in the Bible as "wolves in sheep's clothing"? Should we expect to encounter false teachers today?

13. Ibid., 325. See also WCF 3.1; WLC 191.

3. What is antinomianism? What makes it erroneous? Were any of the biblical writers antinomians?
4. Which example of destruction in 2 Peter 2 sticks out the most to you? Why is it so memorable?
5. Second Peter 2:21 states that Christianity is a holy commandment and a way of righteousness. How does this inform your understanding of Christianity?
6. In what way are eschatology (one's view of the end of the world) and ethics (one's manner of life) related in 2 Peter?
7. Does Peter teach that our world will be destroyed or renewed?

5

Keep Yourselves in the Love of God: The Message of Jude

Beloved, although I was very eager to write to you about our common salvation, I found it necessary to write appealing to you to contend for the faith that was once for all delivered to the saints. (Jude 3)

But you, beloved, building yourselves up in your most holy faith and praying in the Holy Spirit, keep yourselves in the love of God, waiting for the mercy of our Lord Jesus Christ that leads to eternal life. (Jude 20–21)

What Do We Know about Jude?

The short book of Jude has been called the most neglected book in the New Testament. This widespread neglect is unfortunate because it is God's inspired Word to us. Jude provides practical advice for how we are to keep ourselves in God's love and avoid the errors of those who preach the spirit of this age rather than God's Word. As we will see, Jude is similar to 2 Peter in its content and in the nature of the opponents of apostolic teaching, though Jude is more like a sermon than 2 Peter.[1]

A fascinating aspect of Jude is the identity of the author. Jude, in a rather understated way, identifies himself as a servant of Jesus Christ and the brother of James. The James in view here is not the disciple James, the son of Zebedee and brother of John (this James was executed around A.D. 44 by Herod Agrippa, see Acts 12:2), but James, the half-brother of Jesus. (Both Jesus and James were born of Mary, but Jesus did not have a physical father.) This James is also the author of the Epistle of James, which we will consider later in this book. Therefore, both James and Jude were written by half-brothers of Jesus. Significantly, neither author identified himself as part of Jesus' family, but both identified themselves simply as slaves of Jesus Christ (James 1:1; Jude 1). Both these brothers of Jesus were well known in the early church.[2]

As slaves of Jesus Christ, both these men clearly recognize a distinction between themselves and their half-brother, their Master. We know of four brothers of Jesus during his earthly ministry (James, Joseph [Joses], Simon, Judas [Jude], see Matt. 13:55; Mark 6:3), and these brothers apparently did not believe in Jesus during his ministry (Mark 3:31–32; John 7:5). They seemed at times to think Jesus was out of his mind (Mark 3:21). Yet the resurrection of Jesus was an event so profound that even Jesus' skeptical brothers were convinced.[3] We read in 1 Corinthians 15:7 that when Jesus was raised from the dead, he appeared (among others) to James, who became the leader of the church in Jerusalem (Acts 12:17; 15:13–21; 21:18; Gal. 1:19; 2:9). Already in the days before Pentecost (which was around seven weeks after Jesus was

1. Richard J. Bauckham, *Jude, 2 Peter*, WBC 50 (Nashville: Thomas Nelson, 1996), 3.
2. Richard Bauckham, *Jude and the Relatives of Jesus in the Early Church* (Edinburgh: T&T Clark, 1990), 9.
3. We do not know exactly when Jesus' brothers became believers, but after the resurrection seems to be the most likely option. See similarly Bauckham, *Jude, 2 Peter*, 14.

crucified), we find the brothers of Jesus together with the disciples in the prayer meetings of the early church (Acts 1:14). We also read that the brothers of Jesus became traveling missionaries, including at least Jude (1 Cor. 9:5). From their conversions, we can gather that there was something so remarkable about Jesus' resurrection that it convinced even his brothers, who had not initially been inclined to view Jesus as the Messiah.

In this chapter, we will consider what Jude has to say about both the indicative and the imperative in the Christian life. Jude mentions the indicative explicitly at the beginning of his letter (vv. 1–3), and then returns to it in his glorious benediction (vv. 24–25), but it is clearly the presupposition for the *entire* epistle. Most of his attention, however, is given to what we might call the *imperative* (see especially vv. 5–23). Jude gives much attention to how we are to avoid the sinful errors of those who would lead God's people astray. Let us now turn to how Jude helps us avoid such errors.

Called, Beloved, and Kept

In a brief span, Jude 1 gives us several insights into the indicative of the salvation accomplished for us. First, he notes that we are called. This calling is similar to election in that it points to God's work in us before we sought God. When God seeks us and brings us to salvation, he is successful. This is known as God's *effectual call* (that is, it produces its designed effect). Although in the general sense everyone is called to faith and repentance, the good news is that God is ultimately the One who enables our belief, and where he acts it will be accomplished. In the effectual call, God persuades and enables us to believe in the gospel of Jesus Christ.[4] This is encouraging in light of the dangers that

---

4. WSC 31: "*Q. What is effectual calling? A.* Effectual calling is the work of God's Spirit, whereby, convincing us of our sin and misery, enlightening our minds in the knowledge of Christ, and renewing our wills, he doth persuade and enable us to embrace Jesus Christ, freely offered to us in the gospel."

Jude tells his audience they will have to navigate. The priority of God's call in our salvation reminds us that we are God's because of his actions in our behalf.

Second, Jude identifies his audience as beloved in God the Father. The identification of God as Father here likely underscores the beloved status all the more. In other words, we know we are loved by God because we can call him Father through his Son, Jesus Christ. When we are born again into God's family, we come through God's Son. God is powerful above all, and he is able to call and keep us, but he is also a tender Father. There are no beings in the universe greater than our God, the only Creator and Savior (Ex. 15:11; Deut. 33:26; Pss. 86:10; 89:6; 113:5–6; Isa. 40:9–31; 43:11; 44:6–8). Yet God cares for us and sustains us as a Father. We see this in the way he capably carried Israel through the wilderness, as a father would an exhausted child (Deut. 1:31). He is compassionate as a Father, remembering our sins no more (Ps. 103:12–14). Similarly, in Psalm 35:10 the greatness of God is linked with his compassion as he delivers the poor and needy. Through Christ, God our Father is both powerful and compassionate and loves us more than we can imagine.

Third, Jude notes that we are kept for Jesus Christ.[5] *Keeping* is an important theme in Jude and has an eschatological, future goal in view. Christians are *kept* for Jesus Christ (v. 1) and called to *keep* themselves in the love of God (v. 21). On the other hand, the angels who did not *keep* themselves in their proper sphere of authority are *kept* in eternal chains for the day of judgment (v. 6), and in a similar way the judgment is being *kept* for the false teachers (v. 13). In light of such dangers, it is vitally helpful to know that God is keeping us for Christ. We do not ultimately

---

5. This is the rendering of the ESV and NIV (2011). The older (and perhaps more familiar) NIV (1984) translated it "kept by Jesus Christ." Either translation of the Greek is possible.

keep ourselves. Yet Jude also does not hesitate to instruct us to keep ourselves in the love of God (v. 21).

In light of Jude, 1 we also have the prayer in Jude 2 that God might multiply mercy, peace, and love to his people. We may often skip over such statements at the beginning of New Testament letters on our way to the meat of the argument, but these are significant words that reflect on God's blessings to us. Moreover, Jude will return to these important themes throughout his letter, encouraging his recipients to have mercy in the way that God has had mercy on us (vv. 22–23). Additionally, the call to keep ourselves in the love of God (v. 21) assumes that God is the One who first loves us (v. 2), which leads to the peace of knowing that there is no enmity between us and God. For if we trust in Christ, we will be presented before the presence of God not condemned, but spotless with great joy (v. 24).

The Faith Once Delivered

The indicative of our salvation is also in view in Jude 3–4. First, Jude writes about our common salvation (v. 3). There are not varying ways of salvation for different people, nor is anyone inherently worthy to enter the kingdom of God. We share the same salvation that is a gift of God for sinners who are unable to save themselves. The brother of Jesus is in need of the same salvation as you and I. Additionally, this salvation brings about a new community of God's people. We share together in the blessings of salvation, and we are to build one another up in the faith. For example, Paul points out that we have all received spiritual gifts not to build ourselves up, but to serve our brothers and sisters in Christ (Rom. 12:4–8; 1 Cor. 12). Jude may also intend here a critique of the false teachers, whose salvation is not sure, and who seem to be propounding a supposedly better way to live the Christian life, based on their own alleged insights and dreams (Jude 8). If so, these false teachers were preaching secret doctrines that did not come from the apostles, which were therefore something different from our common salvation.

Second, Jude reveals the priority of the indicative by writing of "the faith that was once for all delivered to the saints" (v. 3). Salvation is not something that we attain by our own effort, but it is a gift that is delivered to us. The gracious nature of the gospel is likely in the background of Jude's comment, but this statement may focus more on the way the content of the gospel message has been handed down in an authoritative, pristine way to Jude's own audience (and indeed, even to us today).

How, then, is the message handed down related to the indicative of our salvation? It is because the content of the message handed down deals with the work of Christ on our behalf. As Paul tells us, that which was handed down prominently includes the details that Christ died for our sins, that he was buried, and that he was raised in accordance with the Scriptures (1 Cor. 15:3–4). This is the faith to which Jude refers in his epistle. In fact, the phrase "once for all" may also allude to the once-for-all character of Christ's single, ultimate sacrifice for our sins (Rom. 6:10; Heb. 9:12, 26–28; 10:10; 1 Peter 3:18).[6] We do not earn our salvation or adjust the message, but we simply trust in Christ in accord with the message that has been handed down to us.

This is the faith that Jude writes to contend for. Why must Jude contend for it? Because false teachers had sneaked in and were perverting the grace of God into sensuality (v. 4). The ungodly leaders who had crept into the church were twisting the gospel of free grace into a license to live footloose and fancy-free in regard to sin. For Jude, this is not an option for a disciple of Christ; it was not simply a difference of opinion. For Jude, to live a lifestyle of sexual immorality (and greed, v. 11) was to distort the gospel and deny Jesus Christ. The condemnation of those who distort the grace of God has been established from long ago.

6. Bauckham, *Jude, 2 Peter*, 34.

Before we consider what this statement means, we should look more closely at the false teachers in Jude. The language of Jude is in many ways similar to 2 Peter at this point, and in both contexts the issue of antinomianism (despising the moral obligations of the law) is in view. In 2 Peter, however, the false teachers were scoffing at the return of Christ; in Jude it is not clear that the false teachers were denying any specific point of doctrine. Nevertheless, the lives of the opponents were in serious error, which means that they did distort the teaching of the apostles. This is because right doctrine (*orthodoxy*) and right practice (*orthopraxis*) are interrelated. We saw acutely in the previous chapter on 2 Peter that wrong theological thinking can lead to tragic results. We must be careful, therefore, to believe rightly that we might live rightly. The reality is that the moral aspects of the law are forever binding, even on those justified by faith in Christ. As Jude emphasizes, this does not contradict the grace of the gospel but sweetly complies with it (Jude 4; cf. WCF 19.7).

Thus Jude seeks to correct the scoffers who claim that grace entails no moral responsibility. What is more, the false teachers not only live licentiously, but also (unlike the archangel Michael) blaspheme things that they do not understand (Jude 10). It appears that they even question the holiness and origin of God's law itself! Richard Bauckham provides a plausible summary of the character of the false teachers in Jude:

> Evidently they understand the grace of God in Christ (v. 4) as a deliverance from all external moral constraint, so that the man who possesses the Spirit (v. 19) becomes the only judge of his own actions (cf. v. 9), subject to no other authority. When accused of sin by the standard of the law of Moses or of the moral order of creation, they speak disparagingly of the angels who gave the Law ... alleging that they are motivated by ill will toward men and women (vv. 8–10).[7]

7. Ibid., 11.

We will consider some of what this means in the rest of our discussion of Jude. But at this point we should observe that in contrast to the false teachers who were perverting the grace of the gospel, Jude writes to contend for the holiness of the gospel call. This is of the utmost importance because "it is the gospel itself for which [Jude's] readers will be fighting when they remain faithful to its moral demand and resist the antinomianism of the false teachers."[8] One can see again how closely related the indicative and the imperative are. Jude has made it clear that our faith is accomplished once for all by Christ. Yet that divine work of salvation is at the same time a call to Christlike holiness, and to deny this aspect of the gospel is to deny Jesus himself (v. 4). It bears emphasizing that Jude mentions the holiness of the gospel not simply as an interesting talking point, but as something that is to be contended for earnestly because it is at the heart of the gospel message.

Seven Warnings of Destruction

Let us return to why Jude can say in verse 4 that the false teachers in his day were long ago designated for condemnation. Here, as in 2 Peter, this statement likely has to do with the truthfulness of Scripture, particularly in the examples of destruction we find from the Old Testament era.[9] Jude will explain this by relating the false teachers of his day with negative examples from previous generations in verses 5–16. Jude provides three Old Testament examples of the notoriously wicked and their destruction. Then he points to the destruction of three people who led others astray. Finally, he points to the prophecy of Enoch, a man whom we read about in the Old Testament. We will consider each of these in turn.

8. Ibid., 34.
9. So also Thomas R. Schreiner, *1, 2 Peter, Jude*, NAC 37 (Nashville: Broadman & Holman, 2003), 438.

Three Warnings from the Notoriously Wicked

The Exodus Generation

Jude 5 gives us the pattern of rebellion after experiencing the blessings of salvation that is a fitting parallel to the false teachers. The Old Testament precedent here is the exodus generation of the Israelites. After the grace shown to Israel in their deliverance from Egypt, those who disbelieved were destroyed in the wilderness. A key text is Numbers 14, where we read that Israel did not believe (Num. 14:11); therefore, the Lord was going to strike them (and according to the Septuagint, the ancient Greek translation of the Old Testament, the Lord would *destroy* Israel, Num. 14:12). Indeed, although God did not destroy the entire nation, all those twenty years old and upward died in the wilderness and did not enter into the Promised Land (Num. 14:29; 32:11; cf. 24:64–65). This exodus generation, also known as the wilderness generation, became notorious for their disbelief, as we read in Psalm 95:7–11 (cited in Heb. 3:7–11):

> Today, if you hear his voice, do not harden your hearts, as at Meribah, as on the day at Massah in the wilderness, when your fathers put me to the test and put me to the proof, though they had seen my work. For forty years I loathed that generation and said, "They are a people who go astray in their heart, and they have not known my ways." Therefore I swore in my wrath, "They shall not enter my rest."

As noted above, the main point in this analogy is the danger of falling into grievous sin after experiencing the grace of God. Whatever questions we may have about the wilderness generation, the basic point is rather clear: the notorious wilderness generation serves not as an example of perseverance in faith, but of presuming upon God's grace and living lives of unbelief and disobedience. The result of their unbelief was not the blessing of entering the Promised Land, but destruction in the wilderness.

Let us now consider some additional aspects of the analogy of the wilderness generation. First, note the primacy of God's initiative in salvation. We have been calling this the *priority of the indicative*. The Israelites did not deliver themselves out of Egypt; Jesus delivered them. Jude is not speaking about salvation by our works, but about the salvation that is a gift. Notice, too, that a related point is the emphasis Jude places on *remembering*. As we saw in 2 Peter, Christians must remember the indicative of the past. We must not forget what Christ accomplished for us. Our faith is historical; our faith is founded on and celebrates the saving actions of God in history on our behalf. Jude therefore wants his readers to remember the message they received that communicated this saving action of God to them.

Second, persistence in unbelief, despite the effulgent and manifest grace of God, is a singularly egregious sin. The sinfulness of the wilderness generation is magnified because of the powerful deliverance that God wrought for them in Egypt through signs, wonders, a mighty hand, and an outstretched arm (Deut. 4:34; 7:19; 26:8; Jer. 32:21).

Third, what about the question of the security of our salvation? If the wilderness generation was saved from Egypt and was later destroyed, does this indicate that we can lose our salvation? Jude answers the second part of this question with an emphatic "No." He has already stated that we are kept for Christ (v. 2), and he will return to this notion of God's preservation of his people at the end of the letter (vv. 24–25). At the same time, Jude does point to the wilderness generation as an illustration of the false teachers in his day who presumed upon the grace of God and whose condemnation was sure.

The wilderness generation is a collective example of unbelief and a warning to us not to presume that God's favor in the past negates our need for ongoing faith and covenantal obedience. Indeed, the warnings in Scripture against unbelief are especially strong for God's covenant people.[10] The wilderness generation paints this picture for us starkly. Notice especially that the indictment against the wilderness generation in Jude 5 is their *lack of belief*[11] (though disbelief issues in disobedience[12]). In sum, Jude points to the wilderness generation as an example of the destruction that comes to those who knew of God's grace, but who did not continue in belief. Their situation from long ago is a fitting corollary to the false teachers of Jude's context centuries later.

The Sin of Angels

The second example that Jude points to is the sin of the angels. Here he has in view the same account we saw in the last chapter on 2 Peter. Thus, one's conclusion as to whether the angelic sin was connected with the sons of God in Genesis 6:1–4 will also apply to Jude. I argued previously that we must exercise caution at this point, since the Bible is not clear on what the nature of the angelic sin was. Although we cannot be confident that the angelic sin was sexual in nature, we can say that both 2 Peter and Jude seem to relate the fall of the angels to the dangers of sexual sin. Indeed, in Jude we find a very close connection made to the sin of the angels and the sin of Sodom and Gomorrah (v. 7).

But before we explore further the connection with Sodom and Gomorrah, we should consider what Jude adds to our knowledge about the angelic transgression. In Jude 6, we read that the angels "did not stay within their own position of authority, but left their proper dwelling." What we do know is that the angels

---

10. See, for example, the famous warning passage in Hebrews 6:4–6. The blessings listed here seem to be the blessings of being among God's covenant people. Yet the outward experience of these blessings does not guarantee the inward reality of a heart that is truly renewed and committed to God.

11. So Schreiner, *1, 2 Peter, Jude*, 446.

12. Bauckham, *Jude, 2 Peter*, 50.

transgressed God's boundaries in tragic ways, and are presently bound and awaiting an even greater judgment. As we noted at the beginning of the chapter, the theme of *keeping* is important in Jude. The angels did not keep themselves in their proper sphere, so they are now kept in chains. This judgment is a warning for all who read Jude: just as the angels did not escape punishment when they contravened God's will, neither will those who follow the destructive paths of the wayward escape unscathed.

Sodom and Gomorrah

The third example that Jude points to is Sodom and Gomorrah. In Jude 7, we read that the sin of Sodom and Gomorrah was indulging in sexual immorality and pursuing unnatural desire. More specifically, the fornication of Sodom and Gomorrah included the unnatural practice of homosexual relations. In the account of the destruction of Sodom and Gomorrah in Genesis 19, we read that the men of the city wanted the (unbeknownst to them) angelic visitors (also appearing as men) to come out of Lot's house so that they might have sexual relations with them (Gen. 19:4–7). In addition to this passage in Jude, we know of a number of other biblical and nonbiblical texts that recognize the homosexual nature of the sin of Sodom and Gomorrah.[13] Ezekiel 16:50 mentions the abomination of Sodom, using the same Hebrew word for the abomination of homosexual relations as in Leviticus 18:22; 20:13.[14] These texts from Leviticus are two of the numerous biblical texts that explicitly identify homosexual activity as being contrary to the will of God

---

13. To be sure, there were other sins in Sodom and Gomorrah. For example, Ezekiel 16:49 mentions pride, greed, and disregard for the poor. But this does not mean that sexual sin was not an issue. Instead, we should recognize that sin often comes in bundles, and we may expect to find sin grievously manifested in a number of different ways.

14. The term is תּוֹעֵבָה. See Robert A. J. Gagnon, *The Bible and Homosexual Practice: Texts and Hermeneutics* (Nashville: Abingdon, 2001), 80.

(Rom. 1:18–32; 1 Cor. 6:9–11; 1 Tim. 1:10). Homosexual relations contravene the created order that God established in Genesis 1–3. God created Adam and Eve as male and female, and declared marriage to be the union of a man and a woman who would become one flesh. This is precisely the point that Jesus picks up on when he explains and confirms that marriage is between a man and a woman and is designed for life (Matt. 19:3–9).

It is also worth mentioning at this point, in light of the present state of the cultural view of homosexuality (and even the view of many in the church), that the Bible's stance on homosexuality does not change with the coming of new revelation. In other words, the sexual ethics of Leviticus in this regard are not abrogated or superseded, but are in fact reaffirmed in the New Testament.[15] Moreover, we should not think that the Bible simply includes the outdated sexual ethics of ancient people, since the biblical stance on homosexuality was often counter-cultural even in its own day. For example, in the era of the New Testament and the early church, we find that "early Christian tradition stood out against contemporary Greco-Roman culture, where homosexual practice was quite acceptable and even highly regarded."[16] In other words, not all ancient peoples believed that homosexuality was wrong. Arguments in favor of homoerotic relationships could claim a very impressive pedigree of advocates, such as we find in Plato's *Symposium*. And yet the biblical writers have a distinct view of human sexuality that is based on God's created order and God's revealed will.

Thus, Jude identifies the sin of Sodom and Gomorrah as their disregard for God's law and their preference for unnatural desire. The Bible often speaks of the dangers of sexual sin,

15. See also Richard B. Hays, *The Moral Vision of the New Testament: Community, Cross, New Creation: A Contemporary Introduction to New Testament Ethics* (San Francisco: Harper, 1996), 389.
16. James D. G. Dunn, *The Theology of Paul the Apostle* (Grand Rapids: Eerdmans, 1998), 122.

including (but certainly not limited to) homosexuality, noting that sexual sin can disqualify a person from the kingdom of God (1 Cor. 6:9–10). Those who engage in a lifestyle of rebelliousness against God and his Word are setting themselves up for disaster. One cannot follow Christ while willfully and consistently disregarding the revelation he has given us. To struggle against sexual sin as we follow Christ is one thing; in the gospel we encounter abundant grace that floods over us and washes us clean from all our sin (including sexual sin!). But to embrace sin and call *good* what God has proscribed is something altogether different. Jude's warning in verse 7 is that punishment awaits those who despise God's revelation in deference to their own desires. Let us celebrate sex within its designed context of marriage between a man and a woman, and let us celebrate the grace of God that brings free forgiveness from our sins and freedom from bondage. But let us never celebrate sin in the name of "magnifying" grace. Let us not make the grave mistake that the false teachers were making in Jude.

The three examples that Jude gives in verses 5–7 relate the waywardness of the false teachers with the destruction of those in the Old Testament who rebelled against God. They despised the law of God in favor of their own dreams and revelations (v. 8), choosing the sexual permissiveness of the surrounding pagan society over the biblical standards of holiness.[17] In defying the law and implicating even the angels who mediated the law (Acts 7:53; Gal. 3:19), they end up blaspheming that which they do not understand (Jude 10). Not even the archangel Michael was so bold as to rebuke the devil, but reserved the word of cursing for the Lord (v. 9). Thus, the scoffers claim special knowledge and insight, but are guilty of serious spiritual error. It is always dangerous for someone to claim some spiritual insight that deviates or disregards the Word of God. The New Testament, especially the "rest of the New Testament," is exceptionally clear that we

---

17. So Bauckham, *Jude, 2 Peter*, 11.

are not to trust those who claim special spiritual knowledge that does not accord with and derive from Scripture. Even if it is espoused by a *New York Times* best-selling author, the "light within us" is never to be followed above the written and abiding Word of God. In Jude, the false teachers were claiming super-spiritual insights, but their ungodly lives demonstrated that they were ignorant of the deep, spiritual realities that they were claiming to be expert in. As it is said somewhere, the proof of the pudding is in the eating.

Jude's overall point in these three examples is to warn his audience—and, by extension, us—of living flippantly with rampant sin. The condemnation of the false teachers was as sure as the destruction of the exodus generation, the fallen angels, and Sodom and Gomorrah. Let us not be fooled into thinking that disregarding God's moral law is an insignificant matter.

Three More Warnings: Leading Others into Error

Next, Jude connects the false teachers to three examples of people who led others astray in the Old Testament. This is clearest with Balaam and Korah, but it is also likely the case with Cain. We have seen that the pagan prophet Balaam not only prophesied truly about God's people from Mount Peor, but was also the agent of great cursing to Israel because of Baal-Peor. The idolatry of Baal-Peor led to the outbreak of a plague on God's people in which twenty-four thousand people in Israel perished (Num. 25:9). The implication is that Balaam led God's people to worship Baal at Peor, thus violating their covenantal commitment to worship the Lord only. This is why Balaam himself was put to death with the sword (Num. 31:16). Balaam was also greedy; he was a prophet for hire. This is a fitting illustration for the false teachers in Jude's day, who may have been traveling preachers who were out for money (Jude 11).

Balaam was indeed put to death, but the destruction that Jude highlights is that of Korah's rebellion. Korah (along with Dathan,

Abiram, and On) questioned the leadership of Moses and Aaron and led a mutiny of 250 well-known men against them (Num. 16). Korah and his associates questioned the limitation of sacrifices to the Aaronic priests. They claimed that they, too, were holy and could offer sacrifices. Korah spoke out against the order and laws that God had established in favor of his own ideas. This in itself was similar to Jude's false teachers. Jude's main point, however, concerns the destruction of those who perished in Korah's rebellion (Jude 11). When Korah challenged Aaron, God responded by demonstrating whom he had chosen for the task of offering sacrifices. The ground opened and swallowed Korah and his family (Num. 16:20–34), and fire destroyed 250 men who were offering sacrifices (Num. 16:35). Already in the Old Testament, we see that what happened to Korah and his followers was understood to be a warning for others (Num. 26:9–11). Jude makes a similar point.

Thus both Balaam and Korah led others astray and perished because of their sin. It seems that we can say the same thing about Cain. Jude mentions the way of Cain, which denotes the trajectory of a person's life. The path of Cain is one that is characterized by rebellion and murder (Gen. 4:8). It does not appear that Jude was identifying the false teachers in his day as actual murderers, but the way of Cain can also be characterized as hate (1 John 3:12). Perhaps Jude intends to relate the hatred of Cain to the false teachers, who are out to take care of themselves, not the flock of God.

Additionally, the way of Cain may allude to the way of covenantal unfaithfulness, perhaps even evoking Cain as the progenitor of the family line of covenantal unfaithfulness. In the biblical story line, starting in Genesis, we have the account of two family lines: the seed of the woman and the seed of the serpent. We can trace this back to the promise God gives Adam and Eve that the seed (or offspring) of the woman will crush the head of the serpent (Gen. 3:15). From this point on in Genesis, we read of two diverging family lines, both originating from Adam and Eve. The first place we see the divergence is with Cain and Abel. God accepted Abel and his sacrifice, but Cain and his sacrifice were not pleasing to God (Gen. 4:3–7). This revealed the heart of each man (Heb. 11:4). After Cain struck down his brother, he demonstrated a kind of remorse about the difficulty he would face after his evil deed. God did protect him (Gen. 4:11–15), but we have no indication that he was truly repentant. Just after this we read of the physical genealogy of Cain, which also reveals the spiritual lineage of Cain. Thus we read of an Enoch from Cain's line who had a city named after him (Gen. 4:17) and a certain Lamech who was a bigamist and a murderer (Gen. 4:19–24). In contrast to the genealogy of Cain, we have the genealogy of Adam that immediately follows. This genealogy begins with Seth (who replaces righteous Abel), and also includes an Enoch and a Lamech. The Lamech in Adam's line, however, looks to the Lord for deliverance and is the father of Noah (Gen. 5:29), and the Enoch of Adam's line walked closely with God and never died (Gen. 5:22–24; Heb. 11:5). These contrasts between two Enochs and two Lamechs help us see the overarching contrast in the line of Cain and the line of Seth, which leads to the flood of Noah's day. As Bruce Waltke observes, "Cain's line leads to judgment, Seth's line to salvation."[18]

The importance of family lines in Genesis continues through the offspring of Abraham in anticipation of the Messiah. The promise to Abraham is that all the families of the earth will be blessed through his offspring (Gen. 12:1–3), yet even from Abraham's family we have the story of diverging spiritual family lines. Isaac is the child of promise, whereas Ishmael is the child of the flesh. This pattern continues in the account of Jacob and Esau.

18. Bruce K. Waltke with Cathi J. Fredricks, *Genesis: A Commentary* (Grand Rapids: Zondervan, 2001), 113; cf. 46–48.

Both children were born of the same woman (Rebekah), but they were two different nations, and the older would serve the younger according to God's will (Gen. 25:21–26). Jacob became Israel and remained covenantally faithful to God, whereas Esau went his own way and turned his back on the faith of his fathers, becoming himself the head of Edom, which opposed Israel (Num. 20:18–21). The lines of Jacob and Esau represent the seed of the woman and the seed of the serpent (Mal. 1:2–3; Rom. 9:13; Heb. 12:16). In Galatians 3–4, Paul picks up on the promise to Abraham, focusing on Jesus Christ as the fulfillment of the seed of the woman as Abraham's offspring (Gal. 3:16), and contrasting the line of Isaac with the line of Ishmael (Gal. 4:22–31).

The way of Cain is the way of self-interest, sin, and destruction. It is not the way of Christ or his people. Jude thus warns against the way of Cain, along with Balaam and Korah. Perhaps Jude would even have us make the connection between the reprobate line of Cain in contrast to the righteous line of Seth that leads to the Messiah. Following Cain, Balaam, and Korah leads to destruction. Jude's warning is that we might not be led astray by the sinful lifestyle of the false teachers.

Jude denounces the false teachers in no uncertain terms in verses 12–13:

> These are hidden reefs at your love feasts, as they feast with you without fear, shepherds feeding themselves; waterless clouds, swept along by winds; fruitless trees in late autumn, twice dead, uprooted; wild waves of the sea casting up the foam of their own shame; wandering stars, for whom the gloom of utter darkness has been reserved forever.

Jude could scarcely have used stronger language. He speaks with great fervency to warn his audience against the foolishness of the false teachers and the clear and imminent danger in following them. The false teachers are like hidden reefs that do not appear to be dangerous, but can lead to the sinking of a ship with little warning. (One need only recall what happened when the great *Titanic* struck an iceberg.) "Love feasts" refers to early Christian celebrations of the Lord's Supper—the presence of the false teachers there would turn holy occasions into blemished ones. They are shepherds who care not for the sheep, but for their own greedy appetites. In contrast, Paul teaches, following Jesus, that a true shepherd is to watch out for wolves and do all he can to protect the sheep (Acts 20:26–31; John 10:11).

Thus the false teachers of Jude's day have more in common with the crooked leaders of Israel's past than with Jesus himself. We read in Ezekiel 34:1–10 that God is opposed to the shepherds of Israel who feed only themselves and do not protect the sheep. Jude's false teachers are further described as dried-up clouds that do not provide any water, and are flimsily carried along by the wind and the sea. They are terrible trees. Unlike healthy, fruit-bearing trees planted by streams of water who delight in the law of the Lord (Ps. 1), the licentious false teachers are doubly dead and uprooted.

The Prophecy of Enoch

We noted above that we find two Enochs in Genesis 4–5: one who followed the way of Cain, and one who followed the way of Seth. A statement attributed to this latter Enoch is quoted by Jude in verses 14–15 to speak of the severity and certainty of God's judgment against ungodliness:

> "Behold, the Lord comes with ten thousands of his holy ones, to execute judgment on all and to convict all the *ungodly* of all their deeds of *ungodliness* that they have committed in such an *ungodly* way, and of all the harsh things that *ungodly* sinners have spoken against him."[19]

19. Quotation marks original, denoting a quotation from Enoch. Italics added to underscore the theme of ungodliness. This prophecy is not found in the Old Testament,

This prophecy attributed to Enoch, a man who surely saw wickedness in his own day in the years preceding the flood, is applicable to the ungodly false teachers who were leading others astray. Indeed, they are identified via this quote as "ungodly sinners." It should be stressed that ungodliness does not deal primarily with doctrinal issues (though it does include that), but is primarily focused on actions. In verse 16 we see the ungodliness is also manifested in speech: the opponents are loudmouthed boasters interested in their own sinful desires. We may also surmise that they were teachers who taught not what the Bible really says, but what their hearers wanted to hear.[20] The destruction of the ungodly is inevitable; God does not overlook the sin of those who oppose him. Similar to 2 Peter, this coming refers to the return of Christ when he will bring not only salvation, but also judgment against the wicked. The warnings to resist the false teachers are clarion.

Jude's Exhortations

The bulk of Jude's letter thus far has dealt with warnings against the false teachers, and the warning to avoid their dangerous errors has been implicit. Beginning in Jude 17, however, we find more positive exhortations for how the church is to live in the face of false teaching as we await the return of Christ. Jude begins by reminding his readers of the importance of remembering the past, especially the predictions of Jesus and the apostles. They should not be surprised to find false teachers among them—scoffers who follow their own ungodly passions (v. 18). What they were facing is exactly what should be expected because they were living in the last days.

which has (unfortunately) led many to focus more on the source of this quotation than on the urgency of its message.

20. So also Schreiner, *1, 2 Peter, Jude*, 474.

In 2 Peter, the false teachers scoffed at the second coming of Christ, whereas in Jude the scoffing has more to do with the mocking of God's law.

Today we can also say that we are living in the last days (that is, the time between Jesus' first coming and second coming, cf. 1 Peter 1:20). Therefore, we also ought to expect there to be false teachers among us in the church. These false teachers may look a lot like the false teachers in Jude (and/or 2 Peter), leading others astray by disregarding biblical sexuality, seeking their own monetary gain, despising authority, and denying the future judgment against sin. We should be on our guard doctrinally, with an eye to our church communities, because false teachers will breed division and strife. By having a solid foundation in biblical doctrine, however, we can anticipate the errors that can arise.

In Paul's farewell speech to the elders of the Ephesian church, he reminded them of the importance of right doctrine from all of Scripture, and warned them that false teachers would come in as wolves with perverted doctrine and would seek to lead the disciples astray (Acts 20:27–31). Therefore, a thorough understanding of the Scriptures is key to avoiding the lies of the false teachers. Such teachers may claim to be led by the Spirit and may claim to be offering new spiritual insights, but Jude indicates that if they shake off God's law and scoff at the notion that God has authority over us, they are actually worldly people, devoid of the Holy Spirit (v. 19).

Paul's parting words to the Ephesian elders are therefore similar to Jude's instruction that we build ourselves up in our holy faith (Jude 20). This building up does not mean that we save ourselves; Jude emphasizes God's control over our salvation. But it does mean that we are to grow in our understanding of the content of our faith and be firmly rooted in it. And we are to do this not in our own strength, but by reliant prayer in the Holy

Spirit (v. 20). In contrast to the false teachers, whose claim to have the Spirit is contradicted by their ungodliness, Christians are to rely on the Spirit's guidance into the content of our faith, which is described as holy. Far from being a means by which we accomplish our own salvation, our continual prayer recognizes our constant dependence on God.

By doing these things, we will keep ourselves in God's love (Jude 21). This likely refers to both the realm of receiving God's love and our response of love and obedience toward God.[21] In contrast to the angels who did not keep to their own position of authority and are now kept in chains (v. 6), we are to keep ourselves in the liberating love of God; there is freedom in our holy faith.

We also keep ourselves in God's love by living in light of the return of Christ (Jude 21). Here is another text where we see that the return of Christ is a time of mercy for God's people, not an event to dread. The return of Christ is our salvation and the vindication and manifestation of the lordship of Christ over the world. We should long for the mercy of that day, which will lead to eternal life. And yet the receiving of mercy indicates that we might otherwise receive judgment if not for the grace of God.[22]

Before we look at our attitude toward others, we should take note of the Trinitarian nature of this exhortation in Jude 20–21: we are to pray in the Holy Spirit, keep ourselves in the love of God, and await the return of the Lord Jesus Christ. Jude moves seamlessly between the persons of the Godhead as he explains how we are to grow in our faith. Our Christian living is to be informed by the Trinitarian shape of our salvation at a very practical level.

Despite the strong language in Jude, notice that he ends on a very tender note. We are to be concerned not only with ourselves, but with our brothers and sisters around us. We are not only to

21. See ibid., 481–83.
22. So also Bauckham, *Jude, 2 Peter*, 114.

look forward to the mercy that will be ours at Christ's return, but to mirror that mercy to others, especially those who may doubt and be in danger (vv. 22–23). Perhaps we do not struggle with being fooled by the false teaching, but others in our churches and circles of influence may be wavering. They may be in danger of straying into the fires of destruction. Jude leaves no room for one Christian to scoff at another as if to say, "I'm better than you" or "I can't believe you would think that." The call for those who are more stable in the faith is to lead others to the safety of our genuine, holy faith.

Jude urges us, first, to have mercy on those who doubt—those who are being tempted to believe the false teachers (v. 22).[23] Second, Jude points to those who are in some way under the influence of the false teachers. We are to save them by snatching them from the fire that could destroy them (v. 23). Even if these people have been stained by the sinfulness of the false teachers, they are not without hope. We are not to whitewash over their sin in the name of an "accepting" attitude that ignores their sin and may in fact jeopardize our own holiness. Jude teaches us that God takes sin seriously and that flagrant ungodliness will be judged. For those who may be living this way, we should, with fear and trembling, seek to guide them lovingly to the truth without granting approval to a sinful lifestyle that Jude warns against. We are to be agents of redemption, not judgment. The good news is that there is hope for those who may be falling prey to false teaching: they still may be plucked from the fire and cleansed from their soiled garments.

There is a significant reference here to Zechariah 3:1–5, a text in which Joshua the high priest is clothed in filthy garments (soiled, apparently, with human excrement).[24] In this passage

---

23. Here I draw from Peter H. Davids, *The Letters of 2 Peter and Jude*, PNTC (Grand Rapids: Eerdmans, 2009), 100–106; Schreiner, *1, 2 Peter, Jude*, 487.

24. The Hebrew word translated "filthy" (צֹאִי) communicates this. See also Deut. 23:13; Ezek. 4:12.

Satan shows up to accuse Joshua, who represented the nation of Israel, because of the filth of sin (his own, or Israel's, or both). Satan's condemnation would destroy Joshua and the people. But God responds to Satan that he (God) has chosen this people, and that Joshua is a burning stick snatched from the fire (3:2) who will be clothed with pure garments (3:4). The good news of forgiveness and restoration found in Zechariah 3 is in the background of Jude 22–23: God can easily rescue those whose garments are soiled from sin and who are in danger of the fire of judgment, and wash their sins away. God's arm is not too short to save anyone who is in danger from false teaching and ungodliness.

The Benediction

The good news of God's saving work for us continues in the final two verses of Jude, which constitute one of the great biblical benedictions:

> Now to him who is able to keep you from stumbling and to present you blameless before the presence of his glory with great joy, to the only God, our Savior, through Jesus Christ our Lord, be glory, majesty, dominion, and authority, before all time and now and forever. Amen.

Jude ends his letter by underscoring the indicative of our salvation, even as it relates to the imperative. We are to keep ourselves in the love of God (v. 21), but the real power behind our ability to keep believing is the action of God underlying anything we do (v. 24). The stumbling in view should be understood in light of what we saw in 1 Peter, which is a final stumbling over Christ, the Rock of offense. To stumble is to perish, not simply to make a mistake here or there (though God does also help us grow in those ways). God enables us to persevere to the end because he is the One who can cleanse us from the filthy garments of sin and present us in his presence free from fear and full of joy.

Perhaps the warnings of Jude frighten us, lest we ourselves be in danger of falling prey to sinful errors. What then is our hope? Our hope is in God, who is able to keep us from the destructive errors of the false teachers. Our proclivity to sin is a very big problem, but God's grace is even bigger. Here is good news when the burden of sin becomes great and we are tempted to despair; the promise of forgiveness and great joy before God's throne should give us great comfort as we struggle in this age.

The glory here is *to* God *through* his Son, Jesus Christ. The ultimate goal in the preservation of our souls is that we might be to the praise and honor of God himself. Our blamelessness before God's throne comes not from our being good enough to earn salvation, but through the work of God our Savior through Christ on our behalf. This is good news indeed, news that underscores the priority of the indicative over the imperative. Jude's letter ends as it begins: with the promise of God's keeping his people to the very end.[25]

Conclusion

Jude uses strong language to warn us against those who may slip in and live lives that contradict the holy faith that we have received. Their ungodly actions are a real danger that lead to destruction. Yet Jude is not ultimately a cold, stern epistle, but one that offers us great hope. Jude relates the good news that God rescues us from danger and will keep his people from stumbling away from grace. Let us give thanks for the mercy of God, and let us lead others into the rich experience of that mercy as well. Though we are to keep ourselves in the love of God and build ourselves up in the faith, it is clear that the ultimate confidence

25. So Schreiner, *1, 2 Peter, Jude*, 434.

we have is in God, who keeps us from stumbling and will bring us blameless before his throne through Jesus Christ our Lord.

Questions for Reflection and Discussion

1. Does the call to holiness in daily life contradict the grace of the gospel in any way? Why or why not?
2. What are the two contrasting ways in which we see the theme of *keeping* in Jude?
3. Explain how the "faith once delivered" relates to the indicative of salvation.
4. Is it surprising to you that the early leaders of the church had to contend so strongly for the faith, even from the earliest days of the church? What might be the significance of that struggle?
5. Why is it problematic to state categorically that the Bible's view on sexuality reflected the ancient culture of its day?
6. Why is Jude's benediction such good news?

Part 3

SCHISMS

6

THIS IS LOVE:
SALVATION IN JOHN'S LETTERS

*The life was made manifest, and we have seen it, and
testify to it and proclaim to you the eternal life, which was
with the Father and was made manifest to us.* (1 John 1:2)

*In this is love, not that we have loved God but that he loved
us and sent his Son to be the propitiation for our sins.*
(1 John 4:10)

THE LEGEND OF THE SASQUATCH (that is, Bigfoot) is one
that continues to captivate popular culture. From the famous 1980s
monster truck known as *Bigfoot* (in my estimation, the benchmark
for all other monster trucks), to a variety of recent television programs
devoted to finding Bigfoot, to a recent line of golf clubs, to a slew of
beef jerky commercials that involve pulling pranks on a Sasquatch,
the legendary ape-man is a continuing source of fascination for many.

One of the most endearing (if unrealistic) stories of the Sasquatch is the 1987 movie *Harry and the Hendersons*. In this film,
the Henderson family accidentally hits a Sasquatch with their

car, and, taking it for dead, strap it to the top of their station wagon and drive it back to their home. To their surprise, the Sasquatch is not dead but arises and enters their house. A series of humorous encounters take place, but it soon becomes clear that Harry (as they named the Sasquatch) is different from the humans around him, and that he must return to the wild. In a gut-wrenching moment (at least for a Sasquatch movie), the family takes the lovable Harry back to the wilderness and forces him to return to his natural habitat, for his own good. If Harry does not return to the wilderness, he may not survive.

How does *Harry and the Hendersons* illuminate the letters of John? Harry had to leave the Hendersons because he was different from the human family. In John's letters, false teachers were leaving the community because, John tells us, they were different from the true believers in Christ. In John's letters, we encounter false teachers who had created schisms and departed from the apostolic community, creating a crisis for the young church. John explains that the false teachers left because they were not really a part of God's people (1 John 2:19). Thus, whereas Harry had to leave the Hendersons, for his own good, because he was not a part of their human family, the false teachers departed, to their own destruction, because they were not truly part of God's family. John encourages his church that the departure of the schismatics is not a cause for alarm, but is an indication of their true nature. As we will see, this historical context has implications for how we read John's letters.

John's letters can raise some difficult questions. In 1 John, we read that those born of God do not sin (3:9; 5:18). These matter-of-fact statements can be disheartening for those of us (indeed, all of us) who continue to sin. Yet at the same time, John writes in order that we may know that we have eternal life (5:13). How are we to have confidence in our salvation if we continue to struggle with sin?

We will see, first of all, that John points to the work of Christ on our behalf. Our salvation is not based on our work of not sinning, but on the indicative of Christ's work. Consistent with what we have already seen in 1–2 Peter and Jude, John is teaching not that our actions are the basis for our salvation, but that our salvation is a gift that comes from God. Second, in light of this indicative, we will consider how John does indeed point to the manner of our lives as an important corroboration and demonstration of our faith. Gospel faithfulness can bring us comfort in our quest for assurance.

Historical Context of John's Letters

To understand John's letters, we must pay attention to the clues that John gives us about the people to whom he is responding. In the background of his letters lie those who have caused division in the church (quite likely false teachers, see 1 John 2:18; 4:1), whom I am calling *schismatics*. They had left the church community and had become the source of great anxiety for John's audience. Difficulties seem to have arisen, not only because the schismatics left, but also because of the sorts of things they were teaching and doing. As we have seen with other false teachers, their teaching ran contrary to apostolic doctrine, and they lived in a way that did not accord with the holiness of the gospel (1 John 1:6).

What more can we say about the schisms in John's purview? There may have been several factions of people promoting various errors, but in general there seem to have been both doctrinal and ethical (or practical) errors. Doctrinally, there were those who apparently denied the messiahship of Jesus and/or the full humanity of Jesus. Thus, they denied that *Jesus of Nazareth* was *the Christ of God* (1 John 2:22; 4:2–3, 15). In other words, they may have posited a distinction between the historical person named *Jesus* and the *spirit* of the Messiah (that is, the Christ) that they saw as a separate entity empowering this man. This disjunction between *Jesus* and *the Christ* may also have included denying the full humanity and bodily suffering of the Messiah for our sins (5:6–7).

Ethically, the false teachers were not living holy lives after the pattern of Jesus (1 John 2:6; 2 John 6; 3 John 11). This is almost certainly why John repeatedly emphasizes that no one who is in the light goes on sinning (1 John 1:6; 2:4, 6, 9). John is writing not only to correct this view, but also to encourage and explain to his audience that the false teachers left the community because they were not really of the true community (2:19; 2 John 7). Their sinful lifestyles were indications that they did not truly trust in Christ for salvation.

We will consider the implications of the schismatics' errors in further detail in the next chapter. Let us now turn to John's explanation of salvation as a gift, something that the false teachers did not rightly understand.

Christ's Incarnation, Ministry, and Death

The historical nature of the life and ministry of Jesus is superlatively important in the epistles of John. In contrast, failure to account for the reality of Jesus' incarnation (that is, his becoming a real man) and bodily experiences was one of the errors of the false teachers. Focusing on the life of Jesus Christ was important to John, because our salvation was accomplished by Jesus in real space and time. The gospel of Christianity is not simply a philosophy of ideas about how to live, but a message about what God has done for us in history through his Son. Since it is best to understand that the author of John's Gospel is the same author as the letters of John, then the letters assume all that we read about Jesus in the Gospel of John. This is not necessarily to say that the letters had to be written after John's Gospel (though they probably were), but it is to say that the sort of information included about Jesus in the Gospel of John (and other Gospels) would have been familiar to the audience of John's letters. Even if John's audience did not have the Gospels in the same format as we have them today, his readers would have known the apostolic teachings about Jesus (cf. Jude 3). Therefore, instead of explaining in detail the ministry of Jesus, John's epistles more briefly allude to the life of Christ, emphasizing the necessity and reality of Jesus' status as the Christ (that is, the Messiah) and his actual incarnation and physical experiences for us and for our salvation.

More detail about the incarnation and ministry of Christ is found in John's Gospel. John opens with the preexistence of Jesus, the Word of God, and describes how the Word was made flesh and dwelt among us (John 1:1, 14). Later in John 1, we read about the uniqueness of Jesus as the Christ. John the Baptist prophesies that Jesus is the Lamb of God who takes away the sin of the world (John 1:29), and Andrew brings his brother Simon (Peter) to come and meet Jesus, whom Andrew believed to be the Messiah (John 1:41). After this Jesus performs a number of signs that reveal the nature of his messianic task, including turning water into wine, healing a man lame for thirty-eight years, and healing a man born blind. We also read that Jesus is the true Temple who surpassed the building of his day (John 2:20–21). Jesus' status as the true Temple explains the allusion to Jacob's ladder in John 1:51: the ascent and descent of the angels on the Son of Man indicate that Jesus is the Mediator between heaven and earth, and therefore a pilgrimage to a physical temple in Jerusalem is no longer necessary to have intimate fellowship with God. Jesus tells us that he is the Bread of Life who has come down from heaven, and that all who partake of his flesh and blood (referring in some sense to his substitutionary death) will have eternal life (John 6:33, 51–58). Jesus is also the One who has the divine authority to grant life, which is revealed by his healing and working on the Sabbath (John 5:15–21), and raising Lazarus from the dead (John 11:25–26, 43–44).

The signs of Jesus' messiahship are found in John 1–12, with Jesus moving toward the cross more explicitly beginning in John 13. From this point, Jesus is more focused on explaining his impending suffering and exaltation, and the need to believe in him when he departs. John's Gospel makes it abundantly clear that the suffering of Jesus on the cross was not incidental to his work, but was at the very heart of what he came to do. Though his death may have been viewed by the world as a defeat, Jesus has a very different view because he has overcome the world through his death and resurrection. John records this for us very pithily, as we find Jesus saying that when he is lifted up from the earth, he will draw all men to himself (John 12:32). We find a double entendre here, as we often do in John's Gospel. On the one hand, to be lifted up from the earth refers to the sort of death that Jesus would die by being lifted up on the cross. On the other hand, crucifixion would not be his ultimate defeat, because Jesus would be lifted up from the earth on the other side of the cross to the right hand of God in his resurrection and ascension. Jesus accomplishes all these things in his incarnation. To deny the significance of his substitutionary suffering and death (as the schismatics did) was to deny the message of the Christian faith.

In light of the challenge of the schismatics, John opens his first epistle with a reference to the incarnation of Jesus. The first two verses read:

> That which was from the beginning, which we have heard, which we have seen with our eyes, which we looked upon and have touched with our hands, concerning the word of life—the life was made manifest, and we have seen it, and testify to it and proclaim to you the eternal life, which was with the Father and was made manifest to us. (1 John 1:1–2)

Although this may sound a bit like impersonal language, John is referring to the person of Jesus, who has really come in the flesh and therefore could be seen, touched, and heard. The language is about the Word made flesh, Jesus Christ himself (John 1:1, 14). The reality of the salvation accomplished by Jesus in his incarnation provides the presupposition for John's letters.

The incarnation as described in 1 John 1 also assumes that the Son of God existed before he became a man. Thus, "that which was from the beginning" refers to the eternal Son, who, in the fullness of time, was born of a woman, born under the law (Gal. 4:4). John emphasizes the physicality of the incarnation because the schismatics were denying the physical reality of Jesus Christ and his suffering in the flesh. For the schismatics, these were not important. In response, John underscores the necessity of the physical suffering of Jesus for our sin; Jesus came in the flesh and could be seen, touched, and heard. Additionally, John reassures his audience that he himself is an eyewitness who has seen and experienced Jesus, and John can testify that Jesus' actual, bodily incarnation is true. At its core, the gospel is a message about the life of Christ and what he has accomplished for us. By denying the key tenets of Jesus' incarnate work, the schismatics were denying the message of Christianity.

It is also significant that John identifies Jesus as the Word of Life. The concept of life is an important one throughout John's writings. John 1:4 describes Jesus as the source of life and the light of men, and the promise of eternal life is prominent in John (3:15–16, 36; 4:14, 36; 5:24, 29, 39; 6:27, 35, 47, 68; 10:10, 28; 11:25–26; 12:25; 14:6; 17:3; 20:31). In concert with the Gospel of John, we read in 1 John that Jesus is the Word of Life and eternal life (1:1–2), he promises us eternal life (2:25), in him is life (5:11), and he keeps us for eternal life (5:18). John thus emphasizes the indicative of our salvation by focusing on the life that Jesus offers to us, the life that can be found only in Jesus himself. We cannot bypass

Jesus to receive life. Jesus even rebukes some of his opponents for thinking they could have life in the holy Scriptures apart from him! "You search the Scriptures because you think that in them you have eternal life; and it is they that bear witness about me, yet you refuse to come to me that you may have life" (John 5:39–40). Surely, they may have thought, that life is found in knowing and following the words of God. Yet Jesus responds in no uncertain terms that the Scriptures point us to him, and that to miss the focus on Jesus in Scripture is to miss the life that Scripture offers us. Here is a warning for all who study Scripture: may we never allow knowledge of the Bible to occlude the reality and glory of Christ, whom we meet on its pages.

Recognizing the fundamental point that life does not reside in ourselves, but in Christ, allows us to consider a key aspect of salvation. According to 1 John, our salvation comes from outside ourselves (Latin: *extra nos*). The life to which we aspire comes not *from within*, but *from without*. To look for life, we therefore look not to ourselves, whether it be to our own walking in the light or our own following in obedience. Instead, we look to Christ, in whom is life. Said another way, the indicative has primacy over the imperative in John's discussion of salvation.

Another text in 1 John that discusses the importance of Jesus' incarnation is 5:6: "This is he who came by water and blood— Jesus Christ; not by the water only but by the water and the blood. And the Spirit is the one who testifies, because the Spirit is the truth." This text confirms that Jesus Christ (that is, the one person Jesus Christ; there is no distinction between Jesus and Christ) came by both water and the blood. "The water and the blood" probably refers to the entire ministry of Jesus, from his baptism (water) to his death (blood). John's point is that the same Jesus who was confirmed as the Christ at his baptism is the same Jesus who, as the Christ, was crucified on a Roman cross at Calvary. In contrast to the schismatics, who eschewed or at least downplayed the notion of a suffering Messiah, John shows us that a suffering and crucified Messiah is not an embarrassment to be avoided, but a necessity to cleanse us from sin (1 John 1:7).

Christ's Death as Propitiation

The necessity of Jesus' death on the cross is revealed by the term that John uses to describe it: *propitiation* (1 John 2:2; 4:10). This theological term is worth adopting into our vocabulary, since it communicates something essential about the gospel. By using the term *propitiation*, John shows us that the death of Christ satisfies the wrath of God against sin. Consequently, it also reminds us that sin is a serious affront to the holiness of God. A denial of the gravity of sin likely underlies the lax attitude toward licentiousness that we saw in the opponents of 2 Peter and Jude, and this mind-set likely also characterizes the schismatics to whom John responds. As sinners, we are naturally in a position of misery and condemnation under God's disfavor because of our rebellion against God's law. As we have noted in a previous chapter, to oppose God's law is to oppose God himself; sin is rebellion against God himself because sin is any lack of conformity unto or transgression of the law of God (WSC 14).

Christ had to come and suffer in the flesh because of the reality of sin's curse. He was made a curse for us, that we might receive the blessing through him (Gal. 3:13–14). He had to bear the wrath of sin for his people for the sentence of condemnation to be lifted. John also emphasizes the necessity of Christ's death in his Gospel. In John 3, we read that God did not send his Son into the world to condemn the world, but sent his Son into the world to save the world. All those who believe in Jesus are not condemned, though all those who do not trust in Christ remain under condemnation because they have not believed in the only one who can take away the curse of sin (John 3:17–18). The good news is that Jesus is our propitiation who takes away the wrath of God that we deserve because of our sin. Thus, the physical suffering of Jesus on the cross as our propitiation is at the heart of the gospel. Since the curse of sin was brought about by a real man (Adam), the curse of sin must also be reversed by a real man (Jesus; 1 Cor. 15:21). Yet only One who is by nature God can bring us to everlasting salvation. Thus it was fitting that Jesus Christ is both truly man and truly God.

Perhaps for some, the need of propitiation to satisfy God's wrath against sin makes God seem like an angry tyrant. Unfortunately, many have reached this conclusion by misconstruing the biblical teaching. We can say several things in response to this mistaken view. First, the problem of sin is not a problem with God, but a problem with us. The holiness of God is not sacrificed because we have broken his law, nor is the holiness of God contradictory to God's love. The punishment meted out against us is a problem that humanity brought on itself.

Second, we must not set the love of God against the holiness of God (holiness is the principle on which God punishes sin).[1] We noted in an earlier chapter the *simplicity* of God (i.e., the doctrine that God cannot be divided), which also helps us understand the attributes of God. God's love is not in competition with God's holiness, but these two attributes (along with all the other attributes of God) are in perfect harmony. We can certainly discuss different attributes of God, but we must also recognize that "each attribute is identical with [God's] being."[2] Thus, it would not be appropriate to set God's holiness or wrath against his love, as if we could siphon off various portions of God's being from others. We dare not seek to describe God in a way that would make his attributes a garbled cacophony.

---

1. Herman Bavinck, *Reformed Dogmatics*, vol. 2, *God and Creation*, ed. John Bolt, trans. John Vriend (Grand Rapids: Baker Academic, 2004), 220.
2. Ibid., 118.

Third, and building on the previous point, let us not over-look the significant fact that Christ as the propitiation for our sin is God's idea, arising out of his inestimable love for us. It is most emphatically not true, as some may suppose, that Jesus is loving, but his Father is angry and vindictive. A key text here is 1 John 4:10: "In this is love, not that we have loved God but that he loved us and sent his Son to be the propitiation for our sins." A few verses later we read that God sent his Son to be the Savior of the world (4:14). The love of God takes the initiative; we love because God first loved us (4:19). New Testament scholar Leon Morris summarized propitiation and God's love well in a classic work: "It is the combination of the deep love for the sinner and the reaction against sin which brings about the situation in which the Bible refers to propitiation."[3]

John's emphasis on the propitiation of Christ also under-scores the dangers of the Christological deficiencies of the false teachers. For them to deny the physical suffering of Christ was to deny something central to the gospel: the shedding of blood for the forgiveness of our sins (cf. Heb. 9:22). The schis-matics' theological errors on the nature of the atonement had then (as they do today) serious consequences. John would have us understand the critical importance of the atonement of Christ. Jesus' propitiation shows us God's holiness and anger against sin, yet it also points us to the deep love of God to send his Son as the answer to the quandary of the wrath induced by our rebellion. To deny Christ as the propitiation for our sins is to deny the only means we have to be reconciled to God and inherit eternal life. John's emphasis on Jesus as our propitiation means that the blood of Jesus washes us from our sin and further underscores the priority of the indicative in our salvation.

3. Leon Morris, *The Apostolic Preaching of the Cross* (Grand Rapids: Eerdmans, 1955), 183.

The Gift of New Birth

Another way in which we see the love of God for us in 1 John is in the gift of the new birth that he grants us. Jesus talks about the new birth with Nicodemus in John 3, stating that anyone who wants to see the kingdom of God must be born again. The logic of this analogy is that the new birth is not something that we do, but something that happens to us. This is indeed what we have already seen in 1 Peter 1:3, and it is what we also find in 1 John 3:1: "See what kind of love the Father has given to us, that we should be called children of God; and so we are." The new birth is a gift that God gives us, and is another way to instruct us that salvation comes from outside us (*extra nos*). Being called children of God is proof of the profundity of paternal love that God has for us. And we will see in the next chapter that if we are indeed born into God's family, we can be confident that we will reflect our Father's character (1 John 3:9; 5:18).

We may also see an indication of the gift of new birth in 2 John 1, where the addressees are identified as the elect lady and her children. This phrase probably has in view a local church and its members,[4] who have received the status of children.[5] This combination of election and status as children thus also alludes to God's initiative in our salvation. As we have already seen in some other texts, election is a way for the biblical writers to emphasize God's work in us before we sought him. God is the One who has chosen his people, bestowing on them the status of beloved children.

How do we know whether we have been born of God? We will answer this question further in the next chapter, but a few preliminary observations can be made here. One way to know

---

4. So Colin G. Kruse, *The Letters of John*, PNTC (Grand Rapids: Eerdmans, 2000), 204.
5. See Robert W. Yarbrough, *1–3 John*, BECNT (Grand Rapids: Baker Academic, 2008), 334.

is by whether we exhibit a lifestyle of sin or a lifestyle of holiness (1 John 2:29; 3:9; 5:18). But it is not only by looking at our actions that we can know whether we have been born of God. First John 5:1 puts it rather simply: "Everyone who believes that Jesus is the Christ has been born of God, and everyone who loves the Father loves whoever has been born of him." Here John tells us that if we believe that Jesus is the Messiah, the One who has suffered for our sins, and if we love the Father, then we have been born of God. The schismatics denied that Jesus was the Christ; those who believe that Jesus truly is the Christ are born of God. To be sure, this true belief will lead to true love of others, but the veracity of our belief is a key aspect of being born of God, for it is not possible to love God and despise the Son (1 John 2:23). Put simply, true belief is one indication of being born of God.[6]

Kept by Jesus

We will conclude our study of the indicative of salvation in John's letters by considering 1 John 5:18: "We know that everyone who has been born of God does not keep on sinning, but he who was born of God protects him, and the evil one does not touch him." We must address a key question that arises from this verse: who is the one who protects from the evil one? John suggestively refers to this one as "he who was born of God." In 1 John 5:1 we find a very similar phrase that refers to fellow believers in Christ. While 5:1 could inform the way we read "he who was born of God" in 5:18, a more likely interpretation of 5:18 is that it is a reference to *Jesus* who keeps us.[7] Jesus is the preeminent one born of God, the one referred to in John's Gospel as the one and only (or "only begotten") Son (John 1:14, 18; 3:16, 18). This view also accords with what we have seen in 1 Peter and Jude:

6. So ibid., 269.
7. For rationale, see Stephen S. Smalley, *1, 2, 3 John*, rev. ed., WBC 51 (Nashville: Thomas Nelson, 2007), 289–90.

the assurance of the Christian is ultimately not grounded on our own actions, but on the divine work of guarding, or keeping, us.[8] It is Jesus who keeps us.

The Christian's being kept by Jesus also reminds us that a future goal of our salvation is in view. As we have seen with the other letters that we have considered thus far, John instructs us that we live in the time of the *not yet* as we look ahead to the return of Jesus. The *already* and *not yet* in connection with the return of Christ is succinctly described for us in 1 John 3:2: "Beloved, we are God's children now, and what we will be has not yet appeared; but we know that when he appears we shall be like him, because we shall see him as he is." The *already* is that those who trust in Christ have already received the status of being children of God, which will never be revoked. The *not yet* is the glorious consummation of this sonship in future glory. What we will be has not yet appeared because Christ himself has not yet appeared. Of course, Jesus has already appeared in his first coming. John has much to say about this. But the appearing of Christ in 3:2 is his second appearing. When Jesus comes back, we will experience the fullness of eschatological life, and we will be like him in ethical purity.[9] The promise is that when Jesus returns, we will no longer be polluted by sin, which is not the case presently (despite what the schismatics might have claimed). Instead, the state of being perfectly free from sin will be realized at the time of Christ's return.

Therefore, Christians have no need to fear the return of Christ, because for God's people it will be a day of mercy, not condemnation. This is John's point in 1 John 2:28 and 4:17. We are to abide in Christ in order that when he appears, we will have no need to shrink back because his propitiatory death has

8. The ESV translates the Greek verb τηρέω as "protected" in 1 John 5:18, but this word is translated as a form of "keep" in 1 Peter 1:4; Jude 1, 6; et al.

9. Kruse, *Letters of John*, 116.

reconciled us to God. If God has thus loved us in this age with the blessing of having personal fellowship with him, being called his children through his Son, he will not cast us off in the future. We can therefore have confidence in the day of judgment because of the love of God that he has poured out on us in his Son. Indeed, we can have confidence because the Son of God keeps us until that day.

Conclusion

The Johannine epistles are brief, but they have much to say about salvation as a gift that we do not merit. Recognizing the centrality of the indicative in 1 John is important before we consider in more detail the role that our obedience plays in the Christian life. We would greatly misunderstand John's overall message if were to think that our security in salvation is based on our own actions instead of the work of Jesus. Jesus is the Christ who came as our propitiation to save us from the sin that we brought upon ourselves. Through faith in Jesus Christ, we can experience the fatherly love of God, instead of the wrath of God, by being born again into the family of God. The identity of Jesus as the Christ and the nature of his work were being distorted by the schismatics. Therefore, John had to clarify the nature of the indicative of our salvation. The schismatics were also misconstruing the role and nature of the imperative in the Christian life. John will also have much to say about the imperative, as we will see in the next chapter.

Questions for Reflection and Discussion

1. Why was John interested in the historical details of Jesus' life?
2. What does the term *extra nos* mean? What does it communicate about our salvation?

3. Define the term *propitiation*. Why is this an important term to incorporate into our vocabulary?
4. How does the new birth contribute to our assurance of salvation?
5. What are the options for the identity of the one "born of God" in 1 John 5:18? How can this text be an encouragement to us?

7

THAT YOU MAY KNOW:
SCHISMS AND ASSURANCE
IN JOHN'S LETTERS

They went out from us, but they were not of us; for if they had been of us, they would have continued with us. But they went out, that it might become plain that they all are not of us. (1 John 2:19)

I write these things to you who believe in the name of the Son of God that you may know that you have eternal life. (1 John 5:13)

JOHN'S LETTERS clearly teach that salvation is by grace through faith in Christ (as we saw in the last chapter), and yet these same letters can be distressing because of the strong language they employ in reference to the lack of sin. John's letters, particularly 1 John, make the point that those who are born of God do not sin (1 John 3:6–10; 5:18). How do statements like these comport with the view that our salvation comes from God and is found outside ourselves? How do John's statements about not sinning lead to assurance of salvation? After all, John indicates that all he has written in 1 John is for the purpose that we might know that we have eternal life (5:13). To answer such questions, we will see in this chapter that John does emphasize the character of our lives alongside the work of Christ as it relates to assurance of salvation, but this is not the same thing as saying that we have a role to play in saving ourselves. Instead, in John's letters the reality of the indicative in our lives is revealed by the imperative: we can be sure that we are saved by Christ if we believe the truth and manifest the fruit of faith in our lives.

Assurance of Eternal Life and the Purpose of 1 John

At the outset we should recognize that one of the main purposes of 1 John is to provide assurance of salvation for those who believe that Jesus is the Christ: "I write these things to you who believe in the name of the Son of God that you may know that you have eternal life" (1 John 5:13; cf. John 20:31). John's pastoral point is not to create doubt and unnecessary angst on the part of his readers, but to provide assurance that if they trust in the Son of God, they have eternal life.

Key in this regard is the close connection between Jesus and eternal life that we saw in the last chapter. Eternal life is not something that is dispensed in passing as if from a drive-through window, irrespective of one's ongoing relationship with Jesus. Instead, eternal life is found in fellowship with the Son of God (1 John 1:3; John 3:36; 5:39–40; 17:3). Eternal life is found in Christ, and those who believe in Christ by faith—that is, those who are united to Christ—experience the immeasurable blessing of eternal life. We can therefore be sure that we have eternal life because of who Christ is. We see this emphasis in 1 John in the way in which John begins and ends with two significant statements pertaining to Jesus Christ as eternal life (1 John 1:2; 5:20).

And yet this assurance of eternal life is only for those who truly trust in Christ. John writes to encourage those who believe rightly and who therefore live in accord with God's will. The problem facing the recipients of 1 John is how to understand and respond to the schismatics, who denied that Jesus was the Christ and who did not live in accord with God's will. For these people, John has a different message.

Errors of the Schismatics

As we noted in the last chapter, much of the impetus for John's writing (particularly in 1 John) seems to have been the schismatics, who taught different doctrines, lived sinful lives, and abandoned the community. There we noted both doctrinal and ethical (or practical) errors of the schismatics. In this chapter we will consider in more detail John's responses to these errors, with particular attention given to how they relate to the imperative of the Christian life and the assurance of salvation. Although doctrinal and practical errors are interconnected problems (incorrect doctrine leads to incorrect living, and incorrect living leads to incorrect doctrine), for the sake of discussion we will consider the ramifications of the practical errors and doctrinal errors under separate headings.

Practical Errors

The first category of the schismatics' errors to consider is practical. Chief here is the schismatics' claims that they had no sin. Because of this claim, one of John's first emphases is the reality that everyone has sin. To deny this truth is to make God himself out to be a liar (1 John 1:8, 10). Whatever else John goes on to say about true Christians' not sinning, he does not mean that Christians are completely free from the struggle against sin. This should provide the context for how we read the later statements in 1 John that those who are born of God do not sin. John begins the main argument of his letter with a reality check that there is no one who does not sin (1:5–10). The ongoing presence of sin in the life of the Christian is one of the first points that John establishes, and this is most likely because of the schismatics' startling claim that they did not sin. Presumably, they were stating that they were under grace and consequently were not subject to sin (1 John 3:6–10). Therefore, they probably taught (deceptively) that we do not need to concern ourselves with outdated notions such as sin, holiness, and repentance, since the grace of the gospel renders all obedience inconsequential. John writes (as do Peter and Jude) to correct such distortions of the gospel of grace. John explains that a denial of sin is a denial of the gospel message.

John's emphasis on the continuing presence of sin and need for forgiveness is both disconcerting and freeing. It is disconcerting because we should want to be free from sin in all its forms. We know that sin is contrary to God's will and brings destruction and death. We should long for the day when all sin will be done away with, and when we will be free from the pain that accompanies sin. But John's emphasis can also be freeing for the one who seeks assurance of salvation. The reality that we will not be free from sin in this life provides the context for John's later statements that those born of God do not continue in sin (see 1 John 1:6; 2:4, 6, 9). We should loathe the remaining sin in our lives and long to grow more in holiness (something that we all have room to grow in), but in spite of this continuing struggle against sin, John insists that we can have real assurance of salvation. When John says that those born of God do not sin, he refers to the overall thrust of their lives, not the absence of sin altogether. Both our ongoing struggle against sin, on the one hand, and increasing growth in holiness, on the other hand, must be taken into account as we seek assurance of salvation.

A second practical error of the schismatics (which is, of course, also a doctrinal error) is their claim to have special knowledge or special spiritual experiences that supposedly gave them deeper insights into spiritual realities. Several statements in 1 John reveal this aspect of the schismatics. They claimed to have fellowship with God (1:6; 2:6), to know God (2:4), to have seen God in some way (3:6; 4:12, 20; 3 John 11), to love God (1 John 4:20), and to walk in the light of God (2:9). Such assertions would certainly have been intriguing and inviting to others in the church who wanted to go deeper in their spiritual lives. But should they trust these statements? Should they follow these (false) teachers who professed to have deeper spiritual insights? John answers these questions in large measure by pointing out the inconsistency of the false teachers' declarations and their conduct. Their allegedly deeper spiritual experiences did not lead to lives of greater holiness, which contradicted their claims to possess privileged spiritual understanding.

The same is true today. One cannot claim to have a deeper connection to Jesus while living a more sinful life. True Christian experience and fellowship lead to greater holiness because true Christian growth means abiding in Christ. If we abide in fellowship with Christ, we will grow in holiness after his character. Abiding closely with Christ and growing increasingly callous to his commands are mutually exclusive options. Those who abide in Christ do not grow in their love for sin and licentiousness, but grow in their hatred for sin and love for holiness in accord with Scripture. For the schismatics to claim that they had a special connection to Christ, but to scoff at the call to Christlikeness, showed that their spirituality was nothing more than a fancied-up facade.

Doctrinal Errors

The practical errors of the schismatics revealed their doctrinal errors that we introduced in the last chapter. The denial of sin is a doctrinal error that contradicts the clear teaching of Scripture. To claim special spiritual experiences that deviate from the apostolic gospel is also a doctrinal error, since the apostolic gospel is a gospel of holiness. But here, under the heading of doctrinal errors, we will primarily consider three things: the denial that Jesus is the Christ, the denial of the physical suffering of Jesus, and the sectarian or insider nature of the schismatics' teachings.

First, the schismatics were denying that Jesus of Nazareth was the Christ. That is, they were denying that Jesus was the Messiah (1 John 2:22; 4:2–3, 15). John therefore taught that it was not possible for someone to claim to know God while despising the Son of God (1 John 2:23; 3:1). No one can have eternal life while denying the One who is eternal life, Jesus himself. Therefore, we must pay careful attention to who Jesus is, according to Scripture. Jesus is not subject to the whims of our own fancies, but we must confess him according to Scripture. To deny the biblical teaching regarding the person of Jesus is to be disconnected from eternal life.

What then does John say about who Jesus is? He is the One who has existed from all eternity. Although he was born of a woman, this was not his creation. We see, for example, references to the preexistence of Jesus in 1 John 1:1 ("that which was from the beginning"), and even more explicitly in John's Gospel, where we read, "In the beginning was the Word, and the Word was with God, and the Word was God" (John 1:1). Jesus himself declares that "before Abraham was, I am" (John 8:58). Many more statements could be added to these, but the point is that the Son of God is not a created being. His sonship is not something that ever had a starting date, because as the divine Son of God he has always been in a filial relationship to his Father.

Additionally, Jesus is the Messiah who has come as the promised Savior of his people. The saving work of Jesus prominently includes his atoning, propitiatory death for our sins. This leads us to a second doctrinal error of the schismatics, the denial that Jesus Christ suffered for us in the flesh. Thus, the schismatics denied key tenets of both the person and the work of Christ. The propitiation that Christ made for our sin he made in the flesh, and this is at the heart of the gospel message. Belief in a crucified Messiah was not a message that fit well with the prominent ethos of the first century. From a Jewish perspective, the masses were not anticipating a suffering Messiah. Instead, the popular paradigm was that the Messiah would be a king who would conquer all his political enemies.

This explains why Peter, after his epiphany in which he confessed Jesus as the Messiah at Caesarea Philippi, tried to prohibit Jesus from going to Jerusalem to be killed (Matt. 16:16–23; Mark 8:27–33). If Jesus was the anointed King who would deliver his people, why would he then seemingly sacrifice this by dying at the hands of his enemies? The answer to this question reveals something central to the work of Christ. Jesus' messiahship includes prominently the need to die for sins. He came to destroy the works of the devil (1 John 3:8). His death did not mean that he was defeated. Instead, Jesus rose victorious over sin and death and is the Messiah who is exalted over every enemy in every realm that can be named (Acts 2:22–24, 36; Rom. 1:4; Eph. 1:20–23; et al.). Therefore, to deny the bodily suffering of Jesus as the Messiah (as the schismatics did) is to deny a core element of his messiahship that leads to eternal life.

The notion of a crucified Messiah was no less impressive to the ears of those with a primarily Greco-Roman background (that is, the background of those who did not come from a primarily Jewish religious context). We can get a sense for how the Greco-Roman world would have viewed the message of the cross by looking at Paul's letters to the Corinthians. Corinth was a major port city of some wealth in the Greco-Roman world. It was known for its athletic events and high society, and was home to many impressive orators. It was a place where the philosophies of the day wielded a great deal of influence. In today's terms, we might compare Corinth to some combination of New York, Chicago, and Las Vegas. But the message of the gospel that Paul brought to the Corinthians was not one of highbrow elitism. As one leading New Testament scholar has remarked, "in the understanding of contemporary educated people a divine figure would have to be incapable of suffering and immortal."[1] Yet the gospel preached by John and Paul tells us of a divine, crucified Messiah who was put to death in a shameful way because of our sin. The reality of objective sin and the need for Christ's substitutionary punishment did not fit well with the pluralistic culture of Corinth, in which "anything goes" (see 1 Cor. 6:12; 10:13). Paul had to explain how the message of the cross, though it might be foolishness to the world (it is said that the Latin word for cross [*crux*] was not to be spoken in polite company), was the message of salvation (1 Cor. 1:18–31; cf. Rom. 1:16).

Thus the message of a crucified Messiah was not impressive to the schismatics of John's day. It did not fit with popular sentiments of the Greco-Roman world any more than it fit with expectations of the Jewish masses of the first century. The schismatics seemed to hold a view that would have been more acceptable to those having impressive intellectual pedigrees—they avoided saying that Jesus Christ was really crucified because of the wrath of God poured out against sin.

And so it is today. The message of the cross is foolishness to those who are perishing, but to those who believe it is the power of God for salvation unto eternal life (1 Cor. 1:18). The message of the gospel does not sit well with the ideologies of this world. The gospel tells us that sin is a real problem that must be

1. Martin Hengel, *The Johannine Question*, trans. John Bowden (London: SCM; Philadelphia: Trinity Press International, 1989), 71.

addressed. The notion that God might actually curse someone for sin is foreign to many today. The assumption of countless individuals is that all is well and that the blessings of God are automatic. But the cross shows us that sin necessitates drastic measures because in our natural state we are enemies of God. Thanks be to God that he has, based on the great love that he has for us, provided the propitiation of his Son, through which we can move from death to life. In their attempts to redefine Christianity, the schismatics had missed the necessity of the cross, which is of first importance (1 Cor. 15:3–4).

A third doctrinal error of the schismatics was their exclusivistic tendencies, likely related to their claims to special spiritual experiences to which many others were not privy. The schismatics were sectarians; they claimed that they were enlightened with a deeper spirituality, and that only those who followed them could be blessed with this deeper knowledge of God. Yet these claims were disproved not only by their lack of holiness, but by the universality of the gospel message. In response to the schismatics, John teaches us that Jesus is the propitiation for the whole world (1 John 2:2; cf. John 3:16). The propitiation of Jesus is the one propitiation for anyone who would come to God. First John 2:2 also shows us the universal need for the forgiveness of sins. This stands in contrast to the schismatics, who claimed a special way to God, perhaps espousing new and innovative ways to be spiritual. In contrast, John reminds his readers that all are under the curse of sin and that there is a universal need for atonement—the schismatics and their followers were not exempt from this need. The universal call of the gospel and need for salvation through Christ contradict the false spiritual claims of the schismatics. Their way of salvation was for a few; the apostolic gospel is for the whole world.[2]

2. See Christopher D. Bass, *That You May Know: Assurance of Salvation in 1 John*, NACSBT 5 (Nashville: Broadman & Holman, 2008), 84. Bass's title has contributed to my choice of wording for the present chapter's title.

Perhaps some would take 1 John 2:2, which states that Jesus is the propitiation for the whole world, to mean that John teaches that all people are saved no matter what (this is known as *universalism*). But a closer read of John's letters reveals that he is most certainly not teaching universalism. John is careful to make distinctions between those who truly believe and those who only say that they believe. Just because Jesus is proffered as the propitiation for all people does not mean that everyone will come to him (1 John 5:11–13). Indeed, John makes it clear that not everyone who says that he is in the light is truly in the light (1:8–10), and that those who left the community were not really of the community (2:19). We see this in 1 John 3:8–10:

> Whoever makes a practice of sinning is of the devil, for the devil has been sinning from the beginning. The reason the Son of God appeared was to destroy the works of the devil. No one born of God makes a practice of sinning, for God's seed abides in him, and he cannot keep on sinning because he has been born of God. By this it is evident who are the children of God, and who are the children of the devil: whoever does not practice righteousness is not of God, nor is the one who does not love his brother. (Cf. 2:9, 11, 15, 22–23; 3:1, 6, 14–15, 17; 4:1–6, 8, 20; 5:1, 10, 12, 19; 2 John 7, 9)

Jesus is the propitiation for the whole world, and yet not all those who claim to be followers of Christ are truly children of God. If we are to move from condemnation to blessing through the propitiation of Christ, we must trust personally in the work of Christ.

The enigmatic final verse of 1 John ("Little children, keep yourselves from idols") may also be relevant here. It is difficult to be certain, but perhaps this final exhortation is not so much a reference to literal idols (though to be sure, pagan idolatry was a real issue in John's context of ancient Ephesus and beyond) as a reference to the idolatrous teaching of the schismatics. Keeping ourselves from idols means that to follow Christ, we must avoid contrived theological pontifications that do not accord with Scripture.

John clearly has strong words for the schismatics. We see that they were schismatics not only because they had physically left the community, but because they had departed from the apostolic teachings. Put in today's terms, false teachers have deviated from the Bible, which is our record of the authoritative, apostolic teachings. John even uses the term *antichrist* to describe the false teaching of the schismatics (1 John 2:18, 22; 4:3; 2 John 7). For many, the term *antichrist* may conjure up images pertaining to the end of the world, but John indicates that the spirit of the antichrist is not something that is limited to a small time period at the end of history. Instead, the spirit of the antichrist denotes an opposition that will arise against Christ and his church throughout the ages. In fact, there seems to be a connection between the spirit of the antichrist and the church—the spirit of the antichrist takes up residence in the church and would lead the church astray (see 2 Thess. 2:3–4). But this permeation of the spirit of the antichrist throughout the ages is not meant to lessen the force of the term. Instead, we should see that the false teaching that opposes the second person of the Trinity and the divine plan of salvation is no slight matter. It is the most grievous sort of error imaginable.

So today there are many teachers and movements that would use the terminology of Christianity while denying the person and work of Christ. Perhaps they deny the eternality of the Son of God, insisting that Jesus is a created being. Perhaps they teach that Jesus' sacrifice is not all that is necessary for salvation, but is simply an example for us in some generic way. These are teachings that John associated with the spirit of the antichrist, which are opposed to the gospel of God's grace in Christ. There is no power unto salvation if we strip the gospel of its content—even if we use the terminology of Christianity—by denying the person and work of Christ according to Scripture. As we have seen, right doctrine is actually one way in which we can know that we have been born of God (1 John 5:1, 5). Let us turn now to consider several other means of assurance that God has given us.

Four Means of Assurance

We noted earlier that a primary reason for the writing of 1 John is that we might know that we have eternal life (5:13). How can we know? At least four means of assurance are given to us.

Work of Christ

The primary means by which we can be confident of our salvation is the work of Christ on our behalf. John assures us that God is the One who first loved us and sent his Son as the propitiation for our sins (1 John 4:10), and that we love because he first loved us (4:19). Our salvation comes from outside us, and the propitiation of Christ for our sins that satisfies the wrath of God is our primary means of assurance. Jesus is the One who has come by both the water and the blood (5:6), which refers to his incarnate ministry (water of baptism) and his substitutionary death for our sins (blood of the cross). The work of Christ accomplishes what we could not accomplish for ourselves: forgiveness for our cosmic treason against God.

Promises of God

A closely related means of assurance is trusting the promises of God. Of course, the promises also pertain to the work of Christ for us, but it is helpful to consider a variety of promises alongside the work of Christ. One of the clearest is 1 John 1:9: "If we confess our sins, he is faithful and just to forgive us our sins and to cleanse us from all unrighteousness." Forgiveness is straightforwardly promised to those who confess their sins as they turn to Christ, who is the propitiation for sin. It may also be helpful to recall that the schismatics denied that they had any sin. But for those who recognize their sin and long to be free from it, there is the promise of forgiveness. Knowing that God will forgive our sins is tremendously comforting as we seek assurance of salvation.

We also have the promise of eternal life (1 John 2:25), which is given in conjunction with our fellowship with Jesus, who is described as eternal life (1:2; 5:20). Therefore, those who abide in Jesus Christ have the Father and eternal life because eternal life is found in the Son of God (5:11–12). Thus, we may know that we have eternal life because God has promised that eternal life is found in Jesus Christ his Son (5:13).

One more promise that we can point to was considered in the last chapter—the promise that Jesus keeps us (1 John 5:18). Our assurance of salvation is therefore not something that is ultimately about our ability to persevere, but about Jesus' ability to keep us.

The Lifestyle of the Christian

The promises of God, including the work of Christ, are our primary means of assurance. Yet John also has much to say about how the lifestyle of Christians provides vital, corroborating support for our assurance.[3] John provides several ways to gauge our lives by what we love and how we live. Below is a list from 1 John of some of the features of those who are God's children. We read:

3. Ibid., 2.

- If we walk in the light, Jesus' blood cleanses us from sin (1:7).

- We know him if we keep his commandments (2:3; 3:24).

- Whoever abides in Christ must walk in the way that Christ walked (2:6).

- Whoever loves his brother abides in the light (2:10; cf. 4:8).

- Whoever loves the world does not have the love of the Father (2:15).

- Whoever does the will of God abides forever (2:17).

- Everyone who practices righteousness has been born of God (2:29).

- No one who abides in Jesus goes on sinning (3:6).

- Whoever practices righteousness is righteous; whoever goes on sinning has not been born of God (3:7–8).

- We know that we have passed from death to life because we love the brothers (3:14).

- If anyone has the world's goods and closes his heart to his brothers in need, God's love cannot be in him (3:17).

As part of his overall task to provide assurance of salvation, John gives these descriptions of what the lives of Christians should look like. In other words, these are characteristics of Christians that will be evident; they are not unattainable, hypothetical ideals.

Put differently, these are all fruits of being born again. All those who are born of God practice righteousness, just as God is righteous. John tells us that our actions will reveal who are children of God and who are children of the devil: if someone does not practice righteousness or love his brother, that person is not born of God (1 John 3:10). The issue is not, as we have seen, that Christians do not continue to struggle with sin. Instead, Christians manifest a trend toward righteousness and an increasing lack of sin. Christians are not defined by a delight in decadence and self-interest, but we are defined by a delight in the things that God loves and a desire to love others like Jesus. By pointing to the nature of our actions as corroborating means of assurance, John provides encouragement, and draws a line in the sand between true followers of Christ and the schismatics.

The Holy Spirit

A fourth means of assurance—the role of the Holy Spirit— could be easy to overlook, but should not be neglected. Along with the fruit of keeping the commandments of God, we have the testimony of the Holy Spirit, who provides knowledge that God abides in us (1 John 3:24; 4:13). Through the work of the Spirit, we are enabled to confess that Jesus is the Christ, and through the Spirit, we are enabled to love one another.

Summary and Application

In summary, we can say that, according to 1 John, assurance is grounded in Christ, corroborated by our lives, and ultimately tied to the work of the Holy Spirit whom God has poured out.[4] The reality that our salvation is a gift that comes from outside us (*extra nos*) is central to our assurance of salvation. Nevertheless, John also tells us that our obedience is vitally important when it comes to our experience of assurance. If we are not walking in the light, not loving our brothers, and loving sin more than we ought, we may have our assurance shaken or diminished.[5]

4. WCF 18.2 speaks of assurance in very similar terms.
5. See WCF 18.4.

Put starkly, the Bible does not provide assurance of salvation for those who are brazenly living in unrepentant sin. Coddling oneself in sin and straying from the doctrines of Scripture does not yield assurance. This is the way it is supposed to be. Christians are not supposed to be comfortable with sin; it is contrary to our new nature. It should make us uncomfortable and lead us to repentance. Christians living fully in step with the world should not have the same measure of assurance as those who are walking closely with God. In fact, the lack of assurance can be one means that God uses to draw us back to himself.

The good news is that however much our assurance can be shaken or interrupted, true Christians are never devoid of that seed of God that truly abides in them.[6] And as important as our actions are for our assurance of salvation (that is, the imperative), they remain secondary. The primary ground of our assurance is the work of Christ on our behalf (the indicative).

Three Tests of Salvation

Before concluding this chapter, it will be helpful to briefly consider three tests in 1 John relating to assurance of salvation. These tests are helpful guideposts as we think of ourselves and as we test the teachings of others (1 John 4:1).

Belief: The Theological Test

The theological test relates to the content of what we believe. As we have seen, one cannot deny the basic tenets of the gospel message and truly be a Christian, since the message of Christianity is founded on what has happened in history. The schismatics were denying that Jesus is the Christ, and that Jesus Christ had come in the flesh. One cannot believe wrongly about the core features of the person and work of Christ and pass the theo-

6. Ibid.

logical test (1 John 2:22–23; 4:3; 2 John 7). As John Stott has stated: "No system of teaching which denies either the eternal divine preexistence of Jesus or the historical incarnation of the Christ can be accepted as Christian."[7]

Righteousness: The Moral Test

John also teaches us that if someone claims to be a Christian, that person must walk in the light (1 John 1:6; 2:4, 6, 9). Thus, the one who claims to be a Christian will have a life that corroborates this claim. Christians will love the commandments of God and practice righteousness, fleeing from sin rather than embracing it. Those who are born of God do not continue in sin (3:9; 5:18), since Christ came to take away sins (3:5). As Stott says: "any claim to mystical experience without moral conduct is to be rejected (1:6)."[8]

Love: The Social Test

The third test, closely related to the moral test, is the social test. The social test focuses on our attitude toward our brothers and sisters in Christ. Do we love those among us in the church (1 John 3:10, 14)? Do we sacrificially care for one another? Or do we instead seek to spend our resources only on ourselves (3:17)? John tells us that we can know of our love for God, whom we cannot see, by the love we demonstrate for our brothers and sisters, whom we can see (4:20). Jesus' basic command is that we love one another, and all people will know that we are his disciples if we love one another (John 13:34–35). Similarly, in 1 John we read that our love for those around us in the church is indicative of our love for our unseen God. "Since God is love and all love comes from God, it is clear that a loveless person does not know him (4:7–8)."[9]

7. John R. W. Stott, *The Letters of John*, TNTC (Downers Grove, IL: InterVarsity Press, 1988), 57.
8. Ibid.
9. Ibid.

Conclusion

We see in John's letters that our assurance of salvation in many ways reflects the indicative-imperative relationship that we find throughout Scripture. The primary basis for our assurance lies in the work of Christ for us. The good news is not that we loved God, but that he loved us and sent his Son to be the propitiation for our sins. Yet the righteous lifestyle of the Christian is vital for assurance of salvation, because the imperative is a necessary corollary to the indicative. When all is said and done, however, our confidence is in the work of Christ for us. He has accomplished salvation in the past, and he keeps us into the future. Let us rejoice in the keeping power of Christ, and let us be confident in our sure salvation, as we keep ourselves from idols.

Questions for Reflection and Discussion

1. How can it be true that everyone has sin, yet those born of God do not sin?
2. How was the insider nature of the schismatics' teaching contrary to the gospel message?
3. Why do you think the message of the death (or cross) of Christ was often received so negatively in the ancient world? Do you think this message is viewed as offensive today? Why or why not?
4. John says that Jesus is the propitiation for the whole world (1 John 2:2). Does this mean that 1 John teaches that everyone is saved no matter what? Discuss.
5. How does John's use of the term *antichrist* underscore the importance of right doctrine?
6. How do we keep ourselves from idols today?
7. Practically speaking, how can John's four means of assurance provide encouragement?

Part 4

WISDOM

8

THE WISDOM OF JAMES

Therefore put away all filthiness and rampant wickedness and receive with meekness the implanted word, which is able to save your souls. But be doers of the word, and not hearers only, deceiving yourselves. (James 1:21–22)

Who is wise and understanding among you? By his good conduct let him show his works in the meekness of wisdom. (James 3:13)

Be patient, therefore, brothers, until the coming of the Lord. . . . Establish your hearts, for the coming of the Lord is at hand. (James 5:7a, 8b)

"HOUSTON, WE HAVE A PROBLEM." This famous phrase, memorialized in the movie *Apollo 13*, recalls the dire situation facing three American astronauts attempting to land on the moon in 1970. Unfortunately, they never reached their goal because of the explosion of an oxygen tank that threatened to leave the men stranded in space. Their only hope was that

Mission Control in Houston could help them figure out how to navigate safely back to Earth. The film dramatically depicts a key moment when the team of NASA specialists in Houston gather together to draw upon their extensive knowledge, with the unexpected task of figuring out how to fit a square cartridge into a round hole with only the materials that the astronauts had on board their spacecraft. Increasing the urgency of the situation was the realization that if they did not find a solution quickly, the astronauts would perish from carbon dioxide. Remarkably (spoiler alert), the NASA crew in Houston concocted a solution, and the module held together well enough for the astronauts to make it safely home.

The applied knowledge practiced by the NASA crew can be related to the biblical concept of wisdom, which has to do with practical knowledge for how to face the particular challenges of day-to-day living. The Bible states that the fear of the Lord is the beginning of wisdom (Prov. 1:7), which means that we must recognize God's authority over us. He is the One who defines wisdom; to be wise, we must walk according to his ways. When we think of wisdom in the Bible, we may think along the lines of Solomon and Proverbs, and rightly so. But let us also not forget that Jesus came as the One greater than Solomon (Matt. 12:42; Luke 11:31), the One who is perfectly wise (Matt. 11:19; 13:54; Luke 2:52; 7:35) and in whom is all wisdom (1 Cor. 1:24, 30; Col. 2:3). It should be no surprise, therefore, that we have much wisdom to learn from Jesus himself. One way to discover the wisdom of Jesus is by considering his life and teaching as recorded for us in the Gospels. Another way is by looking to the book of James, which records the wisdom of Jesus as it is given to us by James.

Just as the team members at NASA had to apply their knowledge to find a solution to an unforeseen problem, James writes to apply the wisdom of Jesus to the particular challenges facing the early Christians. They trusted in Jesus as the Lord of glory (James 2:1), yet faith does not negate the need for practical instruction in wisdom. Conflicts and factions arose within the church. Believers encountered the dangers of false professions of faith and the need to understand what it means to be followers of Jesus who believe in salvation by grace through faith, while also recognizing the necessity of the fruit of discipleship. James writes to give wisdom to the church living in a tumultuous world in anticipation of Jesus' return.

All of us today are in the same situation. How do we live faithfully in this world as we await the consummation of God's promises? This shared situation makes James a particularly helpful book to reflect on as we consider how we may live wisely each day in light of the work and teaching of Jesus.

Understanding James

James is a distinctive book in the New Testament.[1] It is a letter, but not exactly like the sort of letters we have elsewhere in the New Testament. We do not find the personal greetings and touches we find in Paul's letters, nor is there only one church to which it is addressed. Instead, James was probably a *circular letter* sent around to many churches. James thus does not respond in detail to specific issues in one church only (compare, for example, Paul's detailed responses to the Corinthians), but he provides more general guidelines for issues in all the churches to which he was writing.

The author identifies himself as James, which is almost certainly a reference to the influential (half-)brother of Jesus, who was also known as James the Just or James of Jerusalem (distinguishing him from James the son of Zebedee or James son of Alphaeus, both of whom were among the

---

1. See Scot McKnight, *The Letter of James*, NICNT (Grand Rapids: Eerdmans, 2011), 2.

twelve disciples of Jesus). This James was the leader of the early church in Jerusalem before his martyrdom around A.D. 62. We find him to be the central figure (even more so than Peter or Paul) at the watershed Jerusalem Council (Acts 15) that dealt with how Gentile Christians were to live in relation to the law of Moses. Although James the brother of Jesus is generally not as well known as Paul today, his influence in the first decades of the church was inestimable.

The position of James in Jerusalem also helps us understand why his letter is addressed "to the twelve tribes in the Dispersion" (James 1:1). James was most likely writing primarily to ethnically Jewish Christians. Indeed, we should not overlook that Jesus and most of the first wave of Christians—including James and the twelve apostles—were all ethnically Jewish. But we need not think that James is concerned *only* with those who are ethnically Jewish. Instead, we learn in the New Testament that the church—composed of both Jews and Gentiles—is the New Israel, heir to the promises of Israel. James is less concerned with the ethnic identity of his readers, and more concerned with their posture toward Israel's Messiah. James is writing to those who identified with the promises of God to his people in the Old Testament as they are representatively embodied in the Messiah of God, Jesus Christ.[2] Notice that in the first verse he also references the *Lord* Jesus Christ. Given the familiarity of this phrase to readers of the New Testament, its impact may not be felt as strongly as it should be. By referring to Jesus as Lord, James is declaring that Jesus is on the same level as the one God of the Old Testament Scriptures. This is a remarkable statement to make about one's own brother! James writes not so much to prove this statement, but with the understanding that his

2. See also Richard Bauckham, *James: Wisdom of James, Disciple of Jesus the Sage*, New Testament Readings (London and New York: Routledge, 1999), 16.

readers already shared the conviction that Jesus Christ is the Lord of glory (2:1). We should also observe the close connection that James makes between Christianity and the Old Testament. Christians today are part of renewed Israel; through the Messiah, we are heirs to the promises of the Old Testament.

Additionally, James was likely written very early in church history, perhaps even as early as the mid- to late 40s A.D. James could in fact be, in terms of date of writing, the first book of the New Testament. James can therefore give us a fascinating glimpse into the dynamics of church life from the earliest days, when the church was still largely composed of Jewish Christians. James reveals to us the sorts of things that were struggles for the Christians as they lived after the departure of Jesus to his Father's right hand. The wisdom they needed in the first century is the same wisdom we need today.

Indeed, much of what we find in the letter of James may be described in terms of the biblical category of *wisdom*, broadly understood. That is, the purpose of James is to help us understand how to live wisely in accord with God's will in this present age.[3] Wisdom teaching frequently takes previous revelation given by God and reapplies it for a new audience and context. We find in James that the teaching of Jesus provides the inspiration for James's own teaching. James's words clearly echo Jesus' words in passage after passage, even though he often does not appear to be quoting Jesus verbatim. For example, the following comparison shows how James 5:12 compares with Jesus' words in Matthew.[4] Notice that the ideas are very much the same, even where the wording may not match precisely:

3. See also Karen H. Jobes, *Letters to the Church: A Survey of Hebrews and the General Epistles* (Grand Rapids: Zondervan, 2011), 162.

4. This example is taken from Bauckham, *James*, 92, though I have quoted the ESV. See also Christopher W. Morgan, *A Theology of James: Wisdom for God's People*, EBT (Phillipsburg, NJ: P&R Publishing, 2010), 31–37.

Matt. 5:33–37; 12:37	James 5:12
Again you have heard that it was said to those of old, "You shall not swear falsely, but shall perform to the Lord what you have sworn."	
But I say to you, Do not take an oath at all, either by heaven, for it is the throne of God, or by the earth, for it is his footstool, or by Jerusalem, for it is the city of the great king.	But above all, my brothers, do not swear, either by heaven or by earth
And do not take an oath by your head, for you cannot make one hair white or black.	or by any other oath,
Let what you say be simply "Yes" or "No"; anything more than this comes from evil. (Matt. 5:33–37)	but let your "yes" be yes and your "no" be no,
for by your words you will be justified, and by your words you will be condemned. (Matt. 12:37)	so that you may not fall under condemnation.

Since James is written early (probably before Paul's letters) and since James's wording stands closer to the words of Jesus than to the letters of Paul, when we consider parallels to James, it may be more helpful to look first of all to the Gospels before we look to other New Testament letters. In other words, although James is a letter, it reads more like a compendium of the teaching of James that derives from the teaching of Jesus.[5] By looking at the way James applied the teaching of Jesus to the challenges of first-century life, we are aided in thinking through how the teaching of Jesus is to be applied to our contexts today. In addition, recognizing the close relationship between the teaching of Jesus and the letter of James may also clarify why James sounds different from Paul on some issues; the two authors were writing different sorts of letters for different situations. We must remember these different contexts when we come to the teaching of James 2 on the relationship of faith and works. But let us first consider what James has to say about the indicative of salvation.

James and the Indicative of Salvation

James does not comment at length on the indicative of our salvation in the way that some other New Testament authors do. For example, we find no sustained reflection on the death of Christ as a propitiation for sin, as we do in 1 John. Nevertheless, the work of Christ for us and for our salvation is clearly part of the substructure of James's thought, and he does allude to it in several ways.

One way we see this is in James's emphasis on the priority of God's choice in salvation. In James 1:18 we read that God brought us forth "of his own will . . . by the word of truth," which refers to God's initiative in causing us to be born again. A couple of verses later, James refers to the implanted Word that is able to save our souls (1:21). Although this Word is implanted in us, we should not conclude that it refers to some innate characteristic that naturally indwells us. Instead, the image is of something

5. Cf. James D. G. Dunn, *Beginning from Jerusalem*, Christianity in the Making 2 (Grand Rapids: Eerdmans, 2009), 1129.

that we must receive, a Word that comes from outside ourselves (*extra nos*) as a gift of God.[6] This is an indication that it is God who accomplishes salvation for us. The importance of God's action in our salvation is further confirmed when we consider that the implanted Word refers to the message of the gospel, which points to the work of Christ for us in his death and resurrection. The implanted Word is thus a work that is extrinsic to ourselves. It is also possible that the implanted Word evokes the promise of the new covenant that will be written on the hearts of God's people (Jer. 31).[7] If so, then we have an additional reference to the work of Christ in our behalf, since he is the One who inaugurates the new covenant (Heb. 8:6).

James further states that it is God who chose the poor of the world to be rich in faith and heirs of the kingdom (2:5). While one of James's emphases is the concern that the church should have for the poor in imitation of God's concern for the poor (which will be discussed below), the statement that God has chosen the poor to be rich in faith is also true by extension for all Christians. Anyone who is rich in faith has been chosen by God. All these texts are indications that James clearly sees salvation as a gift of God.

Second, James's view of Christ underscores the emphasis on the indicative of our salvation. Although the references to Christ are few, they reveal that James holds to belief in Christ as our Savior as we see elsewhere in the New Testament. In James 1:1, James considers himself to be a servant of the Lord Jesus Christ, which as we noted above is a deeply significant statement denoting the divinity of Christ. The title LORD in the Old Testament goes hand in hand with the unique, saving work of God, which the New Testament tells us is accomplished by Christ the

6. So also Douglas J. Moo, *The Letter of James: An Introduction and Commentary*, PNTC (Grand Rapids: Eerdmans, 2000), 87.
7. Ibid.

Lord. For example, we read in Isaiah God's declaration: "I am the LORD, and besides me there is no savior" (Isa. 43:11; cf. 43:3), and in Isaiah 45:21 we read that there is no other god besides the Lord, nor is there any other Savior (cf. 49:26; 60:16). James agrees that God is one (James 2:19), yet he can also say without hesitation that Jesus Christ is Lord. This high Christology shows that James and the early church believed Jesus, as Lord and Savior, to be divine.

We see James's high Christology again in James 2:1, where Jesus is referred to as "the Lord of glory." This is a reference to the divine, heavenly glory characteristic of God's own character, which is also characteristic of Jesus as exalted Lord (Phil. 3:21; Col. 3:4; 2 Thess. 2:14; 1 Tim. 3:16; Titus 2:13; Heb. 2:7–9).[8] This further comports well with the view of James 5:7–9 that Jesus is going to return in glory as Judge. The return of Christ assumes his present status as the exalted Lord who has emerged victorious over sin and death in his resurrection and ascension into heaven (Acts 2:22–24, 32–36). Again it is significant to note that James nowhere *argues* that this is true of Jesus; he is writing to those who already believe in Jesus as the Savior and Lord of glory. Their trust in the Messiah for salvation is another way in which we see James underscore the priority of God's work in our salvation.

A third way that we see the emphasis on the indicative of our salvation is in James's focus on the importance of faith. Some might accuse James of being too works-oriented, and others might think James teaches salvation by works. But this is most assuredly not the case. In fact, James does mention faith quite often, with a view to ensuring that our faith is genuine. If we have genuine, saving faith, then we will manifest the fruit of Christian obedience.

But this emphasis on the fruit of works does not mean that James undermines the importance of the inward reality

8. Moo, *James*, 101.

of faith. We see, for example, in James 1:3–4 the need for faith to be tested to ensure that it is genuine. If it is genuine, it will lead to the perseverance that yields growth in completeness of character, with the ultimate goal being the perfection of eternal life (1:4).[9] The logic here is similar to what we saw in 2 Peter 1. James also instructs us to pray in faith, trusting that God hears and will respond to us (1:6; 5:15). For James, the opposite of a man of faith is a double-minded man, one who is not committed to God and therefore unstable in all his ways (1:7–8). Faith is to be focused not inwardly on ourselves, but on Christ, the Lord of glory. Those who inherit the kingdom are rich in faith (2:5), but James also warns us that there may be those who only claim to have faith (2:14, 17–20, 26). The key for James is that our faith is real, and when our faith is real, it will be manifested in works. Faith is vitally important for James. This leads us to our next section.

James and the Imperative of Salvation

The texts considered above focus on the indicative in James. James is deeply concerned with faith, so much so that he warns us against false faith that does not lead to Christian obedience. But to say that James clearly understands and knows the importance of the indicative of our salvation is not the same thing as saying that James's emphasis is on the indicative. Instead, the imperative of salvation receives more explicit attention in James. Here is another indication that we are not being unbiblical to emphasize the imperative in the Christian life, so long as we understand that the imperative is not to be abstracted from the indicative. James and other biblical writers unabashedly emphasize specific actions that Christians are to focus on, and we do well to heed their instructions.

9. See also Douglas J. Moo, *James*, TNTC (Grand Rapids: Eerdmans, 1985), 61–62.

Doers of the Word

We saw in James 1:21 that faith in the implanted Word is able to save our souls, and this truth underscores the indicative of our salvation. Strikingly, in the very next verse James instructs us to be doers of the Word and not merely hearers, deceiving ourselves (1:22). For James, belief in the Word that saves us and the doing of the Word (that is, obedience in the Christian life) are a package deal; both must be true of the Christian. James instructs Christians "to allow the word to influence them in all parts of their lives."[10] The implanted Word is no stagnant seed, but by faith grows into a tree that bears the fruit of the Spirit. The faith that James describes is an active faith. There is no dichotomy between believing and acting on that belief.

James's emphasis on the dangers of not doing the Word recalls the teaching of Jesus. Toward the end of the Sermon on the Mount, we encounter the famous story of the wise man who built his house on the rock, in contrast to the foolish man who built his house on the sand (Matt. 7:24–27). When the rains came down and the floods came up, it was the house built on the rock that stood firm. What may not be as familiar is the application that Jesus makes of this passage. Jesus indicates that it is those who hear his words and put them into practice who will stand firm (Matt. 7:24). To make the issue even more profound, this statement comes on the heels of Jesus' warning that not everyone who says to him, "Lord, Lord" will enter the kingdom of heaven, but only those who do the will of his Father (7:21).

For Jesus, as for James, to be only a hearer of the Word is to be deceived into thinking that all is well, when Scripture states otherwise. Doing the Word, on the other hand, brings blessing. One is reminded here of Deuteronomy's two ways. Long before Robert Frost encountered two diverging paths in a yellow wood,

10. Moo, *James*, PNTC, 88.

the Bible has held out to us two paths—the path of blessing and the path of cursing—and choosing the right one makes all the difference. We read in Deuteronomy 11:26–28:

> See, I am setting before you today a blessing and a curse: the blessing, if you obey the commandments of the LORD your God, which I command you today, and the curse, if you do not obey the commandments of the LORD your God, but turn aside from the way that I am commanding you today, to go after other gods that you have not known.

James stands in this biblical tradition, presenting us with two options. One option is to be a foolish and forgetful hearer (only). The other option, and the one that we should all choose, is to hear the Word and put it into practice. Those who act upon the Word will be blessed in all they do (James 1:25).

The necessity of doing the Word is a particularly salient point for those who know the Bible well and are well versed in theology. Do we really put into practice what we hear? Or are we simply amassing a puffing-up, numbing-down knowledge that does not lead to action? If it is the latter, then we are not wisely walking in the way of blessing, but are foolishly being deceived. Of course, it is not wrong to know the Bible well; indeed, it is most important. But we should seek after knowledge in conjunction with putting into practice those things that we are learning.

The Law of Liberty

The way of doing the Word is the way of blessing even as the law is the law *of liberty* (James 1:25; 2:12). When we hear the word *law* today, perhaps even in theological discussions, we might tend to scowl or grimace, at least internally. Yet the law itself is altogether good. Already in the Old Testament, the law was a law of liberty in the sense that it was given after the liberation of the Israelites from the oppression of Egypt, and obeying the law would lead to the freedom of covenantal blessing. The law itself remained holy and righteous and good, even though it had the effect of leading to enslavement because of man's sinfulness (Rom. 7:6, 10, 12; 8:3). In light of the problem of sin, James may refer to the law of liberty because it is Christ who brings freedom from the curse of the law (cf. Gal. 5:1). For James, the connection between Christ and the law is crucial. When we read that the law is perfect (James 1:25), this should be understood in relation to Christ, who perfectly fulfills the law.[11] Jesus himself said, in no uncertain terms, that he had come not to destroy the Law and the Prophets, but to fulfill them (Matt. 5:17–20).

So the law in James is perhaps best understood as the Old Testament law as it is fulfilled in and by Jesus. This law (along with the Prophets) is summarized and streamlined by Jesus through the two great commandments: loving God (Matt. 22:37–38; cf. Deut. 6:5) and loving our neighbor (Matt. 22:39; cf. Lev. 19:18; Matt. 7:12). These two texts—particularly Leviticus 19—are foundational for much of James's exhortation.[12] Thus, in James 2:8 we read that to fulfill the royal law is to love one's neighbor as oneself (Lev. 19:18). This is consistent with what we find in Paul's letters, where he tells us that love is the fulfilling of the law (Rom. 13:10; Gal. 5:13–14). James describes the law as *royal* because it is the command of King Jesus, who inaugurates the kingdom of God (cf. James 2:5), and love is to be characteristic of the citizens of his kingdom. As Jesus says in the Sermon on the Mount, we are even to love our enemies (Matt. 5:43–48)! To be freed by Christ from the condemnation of sin is to be free to love God with our whole hearts and to love our neighbors as ourselves.

11. See also ibid., 94.
12. See Bauckham, *James*, 142–47; McKnight, *James*, 6.

James on Faith and Works

In this chapter, I have argued that among the themes we find in James are God's priority in our salvation, a high view of Christ, and the necessity of true faith for salvation. I have further argued that this faith is an active faith that produces good works. James does include some statements, particularly on justification, that can be difficult to understand in light of other biblical texts. We read, for example, in James 2:24: "You see that a person *is justified by works* and not by faith alone." How does the phrase "justified by works and not by faith alone" fit with Galatians 2:16, where Paul writes: "yet we know that a person *is justified not by works of the law* but through faith in Jesus Christ"?

James 2:24	Galatians 2:16
A person is justified by works	A person is not justified by works of the law
Not by faith alone	But through faith in Jesus Christ

How can James say that a person is justified by works, and Paul that a person is not justified by works? Both verses are true, yet appear to be in conflict.

To answer this question, we will begin first with James's emphasis, and then connect his teaching briefly to what Paul has to say. In James 2, James is concerned to correct those who claim to have genuine faith, but whose lives do not manifest the fruit of faith. The faith that James is critiquing is not genuine, saving faith, but a theoretical knowledge that makes no impact on one's life. This type of faith does not lead to love for God and neighbor. James refers to this mere "head knowledge" as "faith" in James 2. If someone says that he has faith without works, then what he really has is a dead knowledge that produces no fruit, which is to say that he does not have true, saving faith (2:17, 26). Whereas some might try to drive a wedge between faith and works, James insists that they are inseparable. To borrow language from a popular musical, James shows us that faith and works go together like ramma lamma lamma ka dinga da dinga dong.

James states that works are vital because even the demons believe right doctrine (2:19). The question is whether we are truly placing our trust in Christ, which will be evidenced by the fruit of love. Are we fulfilling the royal law of loving our neighbors as ourselves? Any claim to faith without works is worthless. Two historical examples illustrate this point. The first is Abraham. Though we read that Abraham believed God and that this was credited to him as righteousness (Gen. 15:6), James also points out that Abraham was justified by his works in conjunction with his faith (James 2:20–23). Abraham is a model of active faith that takes the next step even when it may be difficult. A second example of active faith is Rahab, the prostitute from Jericho who aided the Israelite spies when they came in preparation for their attack on her city. Rahab demonstrated her trust in the true God of Israel over her nation's gods by aiding the Israelite spies (Josh. 2:11). Both Abraham and Rahab demonstrate that true faith acts. There is no wedge to be driven between faith and works.

Yet what James says about justification (a term normally used to refer to how we are made right with God) can be confusing. To understand what James means by *justified* here, we should take note of several factors. First, we should recall the close relationship that James has to the words of Jesus in the Gospels. Interestingly, Jesus does not use the term *justify* often, and when he does, he does not always use it in the way we might expect. What we find in the Gospels is that Jesus speaks about being justified by words and deeds (Matt. 11:19; 12:37; cf. Luke 7:35). Does Jesus mean that we are made right with God by what we say or do? Certainly not. Jesus focuses on being justified in terms of the *vindication* or *demonstration* of one's deepest commitments. For Jesus, a person's words flow from that person's heart, so one's words will make clear what someone really believes. The words here are also related to one's view of Jesus: do we confess that Jesus is really God's holy Son, or do we foolishly claim with his opponents that Jesus' power came from nefarious sources (Matt. 12:31–32)?[13]

James uses *justify* in a similar way to Jesus in Matthew 12. In James 2, the loving actions that flow from faith reveal the reality of one's profession of faith. Put differently, in both Matthew and James the term *justify* is used in a slightly different way than Paul uses it in Galatians, though there is a connection between the uses. Paul speaks of the reality of saving faith by which we are *justified* before God (Gal. 2:16), whereas Jesus and James use *justify* to speak of the vindication or demonstration of one's heart commitment. The two uses of *justify* are not contradictory, but they emphasize different aspects of the gospel. Paul is concerned to demonstrate the falsity of the claim that someone can be justified before God by scrupulously adhering to works of the law; Jesus is showing that one's beliefs and heart devotion are demonstrated by one's words, which come from the heart.

Second, it will be helpful to consider the similarities between James and Paul. Though they may use the term *justify* differently, they actually agree on the nature of saving faith. For both James and Paul, true faith must be active and produce fruit. Paul emphasizes that faith must work through love (Gal. 5:6), and that even though we are in no way saved *by* our works (Eph. 2:8–9), we are saved in order that we might *do* good works (Eph. 2:10). Faith and works are closely interrelated in Paul's theology,

13. See Knox Chamblin, *Matthew: A Mentor Commentary*, vol. 1, *Chapters 1–13* (Fearn, Ross-shire, Scotland: Christian Focus, 2010), 671; Adolf Schlatter, *Der Evangelist Matthäus: Seine Sprache, sein Ziel, seine Selbständigkeit* (Stuttgart: Calwer, 1929), 412–13.

but the indicative always precedes the imperative. Both James and Paul cite Genesis 15:6 to demonstrate the nature of saving faith as that which believes God at his word (James 2:23; Rom. 4:3). Both Paul and James would agree that Abraham was not ultimately made right before God based on his works, though James emphasizes that Abraham's works were the preeminent display, or fulfillment, of his faith. A difference in emphasis between James and Paul is found in the way in which James uses the word *faith* both for genuine faith and for inadequate faith, whereas Paul generally reserves the term for saving faith in Christ that issues forth in good works.

Third, the historical purpose and context of James appears to have been different from that of Paul. In Galatia, for example, the church comprised both Jewish and Gentile Christians, and Paul wrote into a controversial context in which a Jewish faction was claiming that all Gentiles had to follow the law of Moses to be true Christians. Paul argues vehemently against this claim, stating that if it were necessary to obey the works of the law to experience salvation, the freedom of the gospel of grace would be abrogated. Since we are justified on the basis of Jesus' work alone (not our own!), it is not necessary for Gentiles to follow the works of the Mosaic law to be justified before God. This would be tantamount to adding our works to Jesus' works. This is why Paul speaks so strongly about the works *of the law*—following the Old Testament law, or any human works, does not make one justified in God's sight. James, on the other hand, is not dealing with the controversy of how Jewish and Gentile Christians live together in the church, since most of his audience comprises Jewish Christians. In this context, James writes to counter the notion that theoretical knowledge of right doctrine is all that one needs to be justified before God. Instead, James indicates that we are justified by *works of faith* or *works of obedience*, which is not the same thing as *works of the law*.

Thus, the works that James speaks of in conjunction with justification are not the works of the law that Paul so strongly argues against in the context of Galatia. Indeed, James's two historical examples of faith that works (Abraham and Rahab) are not examples of those who followed the works of the Mosaic law. Abraham lived before the Mosaic law was given, and Rahab was a Gentile prostitute who lived in Jericho and did not live according to the regulations of the Mosaic law. Yet both are commended for their works that arose from faith.

By way of summary, we may say that James and Paul do not always use the terms *justify*, *faith*, and *works* in the same way.

- *Justify*: Paul uses *justify* in connection with genuine faith in Christ, whereby one can move from condemnation to acceptance before God. James uses *justify* to indicate the manifestation of one's confession of faith.

- *Faith*: James does speak of genuine faith in some passages, but he also warns against an inadequate faith of only knowledge, with no works. This inadequate faith is not the true faith that Paul praises.

- *Works*: The works that Paul condemns are works of the Mosaic law, and by extension any human works; no work can make one right before God. James speaks positively of the necessity of works of obedience that flow from the heart of faith in God.

Perhaps J. Gresham Machen summarized it best: "as the faith which James condemns is different from the faith which Paul commends, so also the works which James commends are different from the works which Paul condemns."[14]

14. *The New Testament: An Introduction to Its Literature and History* (Edinburgh and Carlisle, PA: Banner of Truth, 1976), 239.

The Wisdom of James for Today

We have said that James deals with wisdom for how we are to live, which is a very practical thing. Wisdom has to do with our behavior on a day-to-day basis.[15] Into what areas of life does James specifically speak? We cannot rehearse all that he says, but below are some reflections on specific issues, as we think about what it means to follow Christ in today's world. We should think through these directives in light of the overarching command that is so prevalent in James: to love our neighbors as we love ourselves.[16] Additionally, we would be severely mistaken to view what James gives us merely as good advice. Rather, what he gives us is nothing less than authoritative commands from an apostle of Christ that are to be followed at all costs: "The substance of [the key themes of James is] life and death (1:12–15), and James's intent in using them is to draw his readers into the world that leads to life and away from the world that leads to death."[17]

Wisdom and Temptation

In general terms, James imparts wisdom concerning the nature of temptation (1:13–15). Temptation comes not from God, but from our own sinful desires. Let us not be deceived: the temptations, which appear to promise life to us, in the end lead to death. We have seen this principle elsewhere in our study, but it bears repeating: sin is deceitful and leads to destruction, not to blessing. The progression in 1:15 is clear: our own desires lead to sin, and when sin is fully grown, it leads to death. Therefore, let us persevere in the midst of temptation, refusing by God's grace to give in (1:12). For if we persevere in holiness, the prize laid out before us is the crown of eternal life, and this is no

15. So also Moo, *James*, PNTC, 33.
16. See also Bauckham, *James*, 143.
17. McKnight, *James*, 41.

empty promise; God is always faithful to his Word. The wisdom of James reminds us that perseverance in the midst of temptation is worth it.

Wisdom and Worldly Favoritism

James has much to say about the problem of showing favoritism (or worldliness) in the church, particularly as it relates to one's financial status. In 2:1, James states that we are to show no partiality to those who have great wealth and are more honorable in the eyes of the world. Indeed, James points out that favoritism toward the rich is inimical to the gospel itself, since God has seen fit to choose the poor to be rich in faith and heirs of the kingdom (2:5). The rich do not have a greater status in the kingdom, and in fact, the gospel is often described as the gospel of the *poor*, a state that is illustrative and indicative of one's dependence on God for salvation (Luke 4:18; cf. Deut. 15; Ps. 68:5; Matt. 5:3; Luke 6:20). The church therefore has strong theological reasons to love and care for the poor. The message of the kingdom of God includes an element of reversal and surprise: the poor are often favored more than the rich and powerful. Richard Bauckham observes:

> What [James] requires is behavior consistent with God's choice of the poor as the heirs of the kingdom. The poor are the paradigm heirs of the kingdom, paradigmatic both in their lack of social status and economic security and in the wholehearted dependence on God in faith that accompanies it.[18]

How, then, practically are we not to show favoritism? The rich are not to receive preferred treatment to the poor in the church (James 2:2–4). We are all under the same authority and in need of the same Savior. To put it another way, the rich are not to be treated as celebrities in the church. Could it be that some

18. Bauckham, *James*, 102.

showed favoritism to the wealthy because they were looking to gain something for themselves?[19] Additionally, if there are those among us who are in need, we ought to help them in practical ways (2:16). We should also be warned that friendship with this world (and with the money of this world) is enmity with God (4:4).

This is something to take note of in a celebrity-driven culture dominated on many fronts by mass media. Are we in the church seeking to be accepted by the world and its standards? Do we seek first the approval of God or the approval of websites, newspapers, and TV personalities that may not reflect the priorities of God? Do our sentiments most often line up with those of the world, or with the truths of Scripture? These proclivities can all be related back to the favoritism that we may be inclined to show to the rich, if we are living according to the world's standards and not according to the wisdom of James.

Wisdom and Our Words

James echoes a prominent concern of wisdom literature in his focus on our speech (1:19, 26; 3:1–12; 5:12). Our words are important because they reveal our hearts (cf. 1:26; 3:14). Jesus emphasized this close relationship between our words and our hearts, stating that our mouths speak out of the overflow of our hearts (Matt. 12:34). If our hearts are full of the joy of being committed to Christ, they will overflow in words that honor him and those around us. If our hearts are full of anger and pride and self-interest, our words will overflow in bitterness, grumbling, and ire. Our speech serves as an index of our whole moral being.[20]

We should also be aware of the power of words. God's words are powerful and creative (Pss. 19; 119), and the words of those made in God's image are also powerful. Many have observed how wrong the phrase is that states: "Sticks and stones may break my

19. Cf. McKnight, *James*, 187.
20. Bauckham, *James*, 101.

bones, but words will never hurt me." As well-intentioned as this sentiment is, it misses something incredibly significant about the shaping power of words, whether positively or negatively, for those made in God's likeness (James 3:9).

To be wise is to have hearts that overflow with godly speech. Are our hearts overflowing with words of life or words of anger? Are our words being used to build up others in the church and bless God, or to tear others down around us who are made in the image of God? Instead of merely avoiding negative speech, let us intentionally speak words that serve a positive purpose, building one another up in the faith (cf. Eph. 4:29).

Wisdom and the Future

In James, wisdom also entails living in light of the future. The crown of life that is held out to us is part of that future (1:12), as is the return of Christ in glory (5:7–8; cf. 2:1). At this point, we may reflect briefly that all the biblical writings we have considered in this volume (except perhaps 2–3 John) draw attention to the return of Christ as something that is absolutely certain and should be remembered in our daily lives. James fits right in with this eschatological expectation, reminding us that there is a goal to remember in the midst of trials. When striving for a goal, it is much easier to persevere when we keep the benefits of the desired result in mind. This is true for anything in which we are engaged in daily life, and it is no less true for our spiritual lives. For example, if someone's goal is to lose ten pounds, the disciplines of eating healthy foods and exercising may not seem to be worthwhile. Yet when the desired result is kept in view (better health, more energy, etc.), then the difficult steps that must be taken each day can be endured because they are viewed in light of the anticipated benefits.

Likewise, reflecting upon the return of Christ and all that it entails (including, it should be noted, the heavenly blessings that we receive upon death, should Christ tarry) should motivate us to live faithfully in the present age. Following Christ is not always easy; the world seeks to sway us and cause us to turn aside from the path of life. But when we keep the end in view, and remind ourselves that perseverance will result in life incomparable and unfading, any sacrifice we make in the present age will pale in comparison with the ultimate benefit in the age to come. The wisdom of James shows us that following Christ is the most strategic investment we can make in this world.

Conclusion

Although James may sometimes be overlooked in favor of other New Testament writings, understanding James as a handbook of wisdom built on the teaching of Jesus helps us appreciate that this letter has much to say to the church today. James builds on the indicative of our salvation and shows us that our faith must be more than just theoretical doctrine (even if it is completely orthodox and Reformed!). Instead, genuine faith must be demonstrated by works of Christian obedience. We must believe that God is one, and in practice love our neighbors as ourselves. Our hearts must not be divided, but we must be fully committed to serving Christ and to serving our brothers and sisters in the church, as we anticipate the return of Christ, the Lord of glory.

Questions for Reflection and Discussion

1. What does James's reference to Jesus as the Lord of glory tell us about what the early Christians believed?
2. Discuss some ways in which we know that true faith is important for James.
3. What does James mean when he says that we are justified by works?

4. How does God's election of the poor inform how we relate to the wealthy or famous in the church today?
5. What are some reasons why it is not wrong to focus on the imperative in the Christian life? What are some dangers in this approach?
6. When you think of the law of the Bible, do you think of liberty? In what way is the law liberating, and in what way is it not?
7. Give one practical way in which you can apply the wisdom of James to your life this week.

Appendix:
Additional Notes
on Difficult Texts

THE STUDY of 1–2 Peter and Jude raises some questions for the modern-day reader about the nature of angels and their rebellion against God. This brief appendix provides more information about the angelic sin as it relates to these texts.

Who Are the Spirits in Prison?

One of the most difficult portions of 1 Peter is found in 3:18–20:

> For Christ also suffered once for sins, the righteous for the unrighteous, that he might bring us to God, being put to death in the flesh but made alive in the spirit, in which he went and proclaimed to the spirits in prison, because they formerly did not obey, when God's patience waited in the days of Noah, while the ark was being prepared, in which a few, that is, eight persons, were brought safely through water.

At least two questions arise here. (1) Who are the spirits in prison? (2) When did Christ preach to them?

(1) *Who are the spirits in prison?* Here we have two viable options. The first option is to understand these spirits as those who have died and are now in the realm of the dead,

whether they are believers or unbelievers.[1] This option is a possibility, and it explains well the focus on Noah and the patience of God. But the Bible does not normally speak of those who have died as *spirits* but as *souls*.[2]

The second option is to view the spirits as spiritual beings, that is, angels or demons. This reading of the text interprets 1 Peter 3 in light of the angels who are kept in chains in 2 Peter 2:3–5 and Jude 5–6 because of their rebellion against God. If we understand the spirits to be fallen angelic beings, then the point of the passage is that Jesus proclaimed his victory over them in conjunction with his resurrection. This option would align with texts such as Ephesians 1:15–23, which state that Christ overcame the spiritual authorities and has made known to them his universal supremacy.[3]

(2) *When did this happen?* If "the spirits" refers to people who had previously died, then the proclamation likely occurred in the days of Noah. If one understands the spirits to be fallen angelic beings, then the proclamation occurred after the resurrection of Jesus.

Regardless of the decisions that one makes on these points, Peter's main point is clear: Christ has triumphed over every form of opposition in his resurrection and ascension. His humility has led to glory beyond measure.

Angels Kept in Gloomy Chains?

Regardless of one's view of the spirits of 1 Peter 3:18–20, the accounts in 2 Peter and Jude do seem to speak of some sort of angelic sin before the flood of Noah. But not everyone agrees

1. See Wayne Grudem, *The First Epistle of Peter: An Introduction and Commentary*, TNTC (Grand Rapids: Eerdmans, 1988), 159.

2. Though see Heb. 12:23.

3. A third option has sometimes been proposed: that Jesus proclaimed his supremacy to the spirits of people between his death and resurrection, possibly giving them an opportunity to repent and trust in him at that moment. But this view should be rejected. Scripture does not hold out the possibility of repentance after death (Heb. 9:27).

on when this happened, or what the nature of that sin was. One of the leading options is that the angelic sin was a prehistoric rebellion of angels against God who fell with Satan. A second follows a widespread interpretive tradition of Genesis 6:1–4, in which angels ("sons of God") copulated physically with women near the time of the flood.

I have suggested that we should exercise caution about the prominent view that identifies the angelic sin as sexual in nature, since Scripture does not tell us what the specifics of the angelic sin were. We do know, however, that the interpretive tradition in which Genesis 6 was understood to refer to angels as "sons of God" who married human women was apparently the majority interpretation among Christian interpreters until the third century.[4] Thus many in the days of Peter and Jude were likely familiar with the basic outline of the account of angels who desired human women and produced giant offspring with them, though it is far from clear that Peter and Jude believed this.

In order to provide some context, I quote below a passage from the important early Christian theologian Irenaeus of Lyons (d. A.D. 202), who comments on the "sons of God" in Genesis 6:

> For [unlawful] unions occurred on earth, as angels united themselves with . . . daughters of men, who bore them sons, who, because of their exaggerated height, were called giants. The angels then gave [their] wives, as gifts, wicked teachings, for they taught them the powers of roots and herbs, of dyeing and [cosmetics], and the discovery of precious material, love-potions, hatreds, loves, infatuations, seductions, bonds of witchcraft, [and] all kinds of divination and idolatry hateful to God.[5]

4. Richard J. Bauckham, *Jude, 2 Peter,* WBC 50 (Nashville: Thomas Nelson, 1996), 51.
5. *Demonstration* 18. Taken from John Behr, trans., *On the Apostolic Preaching,* PPS 17 (Crestwood, NY: St. Vladimir's Seminary Press, 1997), 50–51. See also Christian apologist Justin Martyr, *2 Apology* 5, along with *Testament of Reuben* 5:2; *Jubilees* 4:22; 5:1–11; Damascus Document II, 17–19; *1 Enoch* 6–12.

Irenaeus is not writing Scripture, and is therefore not providing an authoritative interpretation, but he does give the basic outline of what many in his day believed about the angelic sin (he wrote about 115 years after Peter died). It should be noted how restrained 2 Peter and Jude are, in comparison to some prevailing thoughts from their cultural milieu. Neither 2 Peter nor Jude contains any unnecessary speculation, and we must be careful not to say more than Scripture says on the nature of the angelic sin.

BIBLIOGRAPHY

Achtemeier, Paul J. *1 Peter: A Commentary on First Peter*. Hermeneia. Minneapolis: Fortress, 1996.

Bass, Christopher D. *That You May Know: Assurance of Salvation in 1 John*. NACSBT 5. Nashville: Broadman & Holman, 2008.

Bauckham, Richard. *James: Wisdom of James, Disciple of Jesus the Sage*. New Testament Readings. London and New York: Routledge, 1999.

———. *Jude, 2 Peter*. WBC 50. Nashville: Thomas Nelson, 1996.

———. *Jude and the Relatives of Jesus in the Early Church*. Edinburgh: T&T Clark, 1990.

Bavinck, Herman. *Reformed Dogmatics*. Edited by John Bolt. Translated by John Vriend. 4 vols. Grand Rapids: Baker Academic, 2003–8.

Beale, G. K. *A New Testament Biblical Theology: The Unfolding of the Old Testament in the New*. Grand Rapids: Baker Academic, 2011.

———. *The Temple and the Church's Mission: A Biblical Theology of the Dwelling Place of God*. NSBT 17. Downers Grove, IL: InterVarsity Press, 2004.

Behr, John, trans. *On the Apostolic Preaching*. PPS 17. Crestwood, NY: St. Vladimir's Seminary Press, 1997.

Bray, Gerald, ed. *James, 1–2 Peter, 1–3 John, Jude*. ACCSNT 11. Downers Grove, IL: InterVarsity Press, 2000.

Calvin, John. *Commentaries on the Catholic Epistles*. In *Calvin's Commentaries*, translated and edited by John Owen. 22 vols. Edinburgh: Calvin Translation Society, 1849. Reprint, Grand Rapids: Baker Book House, 1999.

Carson, D. A. "1 Peter." In *Commentary on the New Testament Use of the Old Testament*, edited by G. K. Beale and D. A. Carson, 1015–46. Grand Rapids: Baker Academic, 2007.

———. "2 Peter." In *Commentary on the New Testament Use of the Old Testament*, edited by G. K. Beale and D. A. Carson, 654–68. Grand Rapids: Baker Academic, 2007.

Carson, D. A., and Douglas J. Moo. *An Introduction to the New Testament*. 2nd ed. Grand Rapids: Zondervan, 2005.

Chamblin, Knox. *Matthew: A Mentor Commentary*. Vol. 1. Fearn, Ross-shire, Scotland: Christian Focus, 2010.

Clowney, Edmund P. *The Message of 1 Peter: The Way of the Cross*. BST. Downers Grove, IL: InterVarsity Press, 1988.

Davids, Peter H. *The Letters of 2 Peter and Jude*. PNTC. Grand Rapids: Eerdmans, 2009.

DeYoung, Kevin. *The Hole in Our Holiness: Filling the Gap between Gospel Passion and the Pursuit of Godliness*. Wheaton, IL: Crossway, 2012.

Dunn, James D. G. *Beginning from Jerusalem*. Christianity in the Making 2. Grand Rapids: Eerdmans, 2009.

———. *The Theology of Paul the Apostle*. Grand Rapids: Eerdmans, 1998.

Ferguson, Sinclair B. *The Holy Spirit*. Contours of Christian Theology. Downers Grove, IL: InterVarsity Press, 1996.

Gaffin, Richard B., Jr. *Perspectives on Pentecost: New Testament Teaching on the Gifts of the Holy Spirit*. Phillipsburg, NJ: Presbyterian and Reformed, 1979.

Gagnon, Robert A. J. *The Bible and Homosexual Practice: Texts and Hermeneutics*. Nashville: Abingdon, 2001.

Green, Gene L. *Jude and 2 Peter*. BECNT. Grand Rapids: Baker Academic, 2008.

Grudem, Wayne. *The First Epistle of Peter: An Introduction and Commentary*. TNTC. Grand Rapids: Eerdmans, 1988.

Hays, Richard B. *The Moral Vision of the New Testament: Community, Cross, New Creation: A Contemporary Introduction to New Testament Ethics*. San Francisco: Harper, 1996.

Hengel, Martin. *The Johannine Question*. Translated by John Bowden. London: SCM; Philadelphia: Trinity Press International, 1989.

Jobes, Karen H. *1 Peter*. BECNT. Grand Rapids: Baker Academic, 2005.

———. *Letters to the Church: A Survey of Hebrews and the General Epistles.* Grand Rapids: Zondervan, 2011.

Jones, Mark. *Antinomianism: Reformed Theology's Unwelcome Guest?* Phillipsburg, NJ: P&R Publishing, 2013.

Justin (Martyr). *Dialogue with Trypho.* In *The Ante-Nicene Fathers*, edited by Alexander Roberts and James Donaldson. Grand Rapids: Eerdmans, 1973.

Kistemaker, Simon J. *Exposition of the Epistles of Peter and the Epistle of Jude.* NTC. Grand Rapids: Baker Book House, 1987.

Kline, Meredith G. "Divine Kingship and Genesis 6:1–4." *WTJ* 24 (1962): 187–204.

Kruger, Michael J. "The Authenticity of 2 Peter." *JETS* 42 (1999): 645–71.

Kruse, Colin G. *The Letters of John.* PNTC. Grand Rapids: Eerdmans, 2000.

Machen, J. Gresham. *The New Testament: An Introduction to Its Literature and History.* Edinburgh and Carlisle, PA: Banner of Truth, 1976.

McKnight, Scot. *The Letter of James.* NICNT. Grand Rapids: Eerdmans, 2011.

Moo, Douglas J. *James.* TNTC. Grand Rapids: Eerdmans, 1985.

———. *The Letter of James: An Introduction and Commentary.* PNTC. Grand Rapids: Eerdmans, 2000.

Morgan, Christopher W. *A Theology of James: Wisdom for God's People.* EBT. Phillipsburg, NJ: P&R Publishing, 2010.

Morris, Leon. *The Apostolic Preaching of the Cross.* Grand Rapids: Eerdmans, 1955.

Poythress, Vern S. *The Shadow of Christ in the Law of Moses.* Phillipsburg, NJ: Presbyterian and Reformed, 1991.

Rowe, C. Kavin. *World Upside Down: Reading Acts in the Greco-Roman Age.* Oxford: Oxford University Press, 2009.

Ryken, Philip Graham. *Loving the Way Jesus Loves.* Wheaton, IL: Crossway, 2012.

Schlatter, Adolf. *Der Evangelist Matthäus: Seine Sprache, sein Ziel, seine Selbständigkeit.* Stuttgart: Calwer, 1929.

Schreiner, Thomas R. *1, 2 Peter, Jude*. NAC 37. Nashville: Broadman & Holman, 2003.

Smalley, Stephen S. *1, 2, 3 John*. Rev. ed. WBC 51. Nashville: Thomas Nelson, 2007.

Stott, John R. W. *The Letters of John*. TNTC. Downers Grove, IL: InterVarsity Press, 1988.

Waltke, Bruce K., with Cathi J. Fredricks. *Genesis: A Commentary*. Grand Rapids: Zondervan, 2001.

Wilken, Robert Louis. *The Christians as the Romans Saw Them*. 2nd ed. New Haven, CT: Yale University Press, 2003.

Yarbrough, Robert W. *1–3 John*. BECNT. Grand Rapids: Baker Academic, 2008.

INDEX OF SCRIPTURE

189

5-7—106
5-16—100
5-23—95
6—81, 96, 103, 114, 134
7—103-6
8—97, 106
8-10—99
9—xvi, 99, 106
10—99, 106
11—98, 107-8
12-13—110
13—96
14-15—111-12
16—112
17—112
18—112
19—99, 113
20—113-14
20-21—93, 114
21—96-97, 114, 116
22—115
22-23—97, 115-16
23—115
24—97, 116
24-25—95, 102, 116-17

Revelation
1:7—65
2:14—84
13—42
20:6—41
21:23—66
22:12—67

22:16—65
22:20—17

DEAD SEA SCROLLS

Damascus Document
ll, 17-19—183n5

OLD TESTAMENT PSEUDEPIGRAPHA

1 Enoch
6-12—183n5

Jubilees
4:22—183n5
5:1-11—183n5

Testament of Reuben
5:2—183n5

EARLY CHRISTIAN LITERATURE
Irenaeus
Demonstration
18—183

Justin Martyr
2 Apology
5—183n5

Dialogue
14—67n16

Index of Subjects and Names